P9-DEW-246

PAVILLON DENON

# LOUVRE
# PARIS

Newsweek/GREAT MUSEUMS OF THE WORLD
NEW YORK, N.Y.

GREAT MUSEUMS
OF THE WORLD

*Editorial Director*—Carlo Ludovico Ragghianti
*Assistant*—Giuliana Nannicini
*Translation and Editing*—Editors of ARTNEWS

# LOUVRE
# PARIS

*Texts by:*
Gigetta Dalli Regoli
Decio Gioseffi
Gian Lorenzo Mellini
Licia Ragghianti Collobi
Pier Carlo Santini

*Design:*
Fiorenzo Giorgi

*Published by*
NEWSWEEK, INC.
& ARNOLDO MONDADORI EDITORE

1st Printing 1968
2nd & 3rd Printing 1971
4th Printing 1972
5th Printing 1973
6th Printing 1974
7th Printing 1977
8th Printing 1978
9th Printing 1979

ISBN: CLOTHBOUND EDITION 0-88225-229-1
ISBN: DELUXE EDITION 0-88225-204-6
Library of Congress Catalog Card No. 68-19927

# DEDICATION FROM THE LOUVRE

JEAN CHATELAIN
*Director of the Museums of France*

*The space reserved in this series for the great French museums, the Louvre, the Musée National d'Art Moderne and the Guimet (Oriental art) would alone justify my gratitude, as Director of French museums. The scope and audacity of the project is equal to its usefulness, and the last quality will be immediately apparent to a knowledgeable public: sophisticated art lovers, critics and curators, for whom this vast editorial endeavor will facilitate comparisons and confrontations between objects and works of art distributed through the world's great museums.*

*In more general terms, the proliferation of publications devoted to museums offers, when they are of high quality, one of the most powerful means of combating the major obstacle to the complete efficiency of museums: that is, the general public's distrust, based upon ignorance of the museums' role and usefulness. The material conditions for a greater use of museums have now been met in all highly developed countries. The rise of standard of living and of education, the increase in leisure time, the growing possibilities for travel—all these factors should contribute to creating a potential museum public, not only much larger, but far more varied than that of the past. But in the eyes of a large sector of this potential public, the museum too often seems a secret world, a place restricted to a few initiates where they are afraid to enter in fear of being, or seeming to be, ignorant. Every publication of quality devoted to museums contributes to the dissipation of this fear.*

*However, there is no question, even for those in charge of museums, of considering attendance an end in itself: the full growth of mankind remains the only objective of any real value. But we believe profoundly that, from now on, and still more in the future, the museum will be one of the means whereby man, at the end of the twentieth century, will achieve this growth, while maintaining a balance between his material well-being and intellectual and moral satisfactions. Progress in modern technology frees us more each day from the condition which burdened our fathers, bringing a constant stream of new improvements to man's environment. But this progress is accompanied by growing uniformity, as well as by a moral and emotional drain. Let us take aviation as an example of a modern technique. With ever increased speed, we fly from one international airport to another, but the two look so much alike that it seems hardly worthwhile to have made the trip. And as for the mechanism of the airplane, it is comprehensible only to the specialized technician. This schism threatens every material area of life. Thus we must concern ourselves now with a taste for the humane, so that our children will be able to preserve it in the better world which will be theirs. They must be able to retrace the long efforts expended through the centuries to arrive at the year 2000. We must preserve for them, in the midst of material comforts, a taste for things which are simply beautiful or moving, whether they be masterpieces which have survived the years, a craftsman's humble tools or the imperfect attempts made by a rudimentary machine. The role of the museum is to preserve all those things which bear witness to the slow evolution of man and to his constant search for the beautiful and useful. Their directors must guard against the kind of pride which insists that everything which contributes to the progress and attendance of museums, contributes, at the same time, to the improvement of man's destiny. But museums are the invaluable humanizing elements of tomorrow's society.*

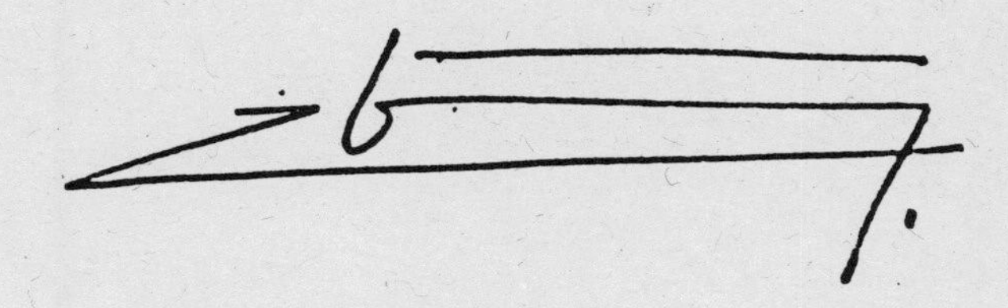

# PREFACE

RENÉ HUYGHE
*of the French Academy*

Culture—by which I mean humanist culture—was born on that day when the Latin tongue affirmed with Terence: "Nothing human is foreign to me." Some twenty centuries later, a painter this time, and a Fleming, Rubens, gave this thought still more resonance by proclaiming: "I consider the entire world my homeland." In every country of the world, the museum, using the international language of art which, needing no translation, addresses itself to the sight, mind and heart of each, echoes this teaching.

The nucleus of any museum is, naturally, its national art, since there is no life force which is not nourished by roots. But as the tree grows and reaches out, it climbs, spreading in the open air, and within this space, sees the circle of its own horizon widen with its growth. And so it is with man. Like the human spirit, the museum spreads its branches, first towards its sister civilizations, then neighboring ones, then foreign, and, finally, towards those most remote and exotic. Its pediment should be inscribed with the words of Rubens, with this slight change: "I consider the entire world my culture."

If there is one museum which can unquestionably make such a proclamation of faith, it is the Louvre. Fruit of French civilization, this crossroads where all races—Mediterranean, Northern and Eastern—have mingled, always has stood for openness and mutual understanding. The Louvre has always resisted the modern tendency towards specialization; within this immense palace whose arms enfold the grassy Tuileries, reaching to the far side of the Place de la Concorde, to the Jeu de Paume, where the Impressionists are hung, it houses the treasure of centuries and nations. Beginning with ancient Egypt, at the moment when an agrarian civilization emerged from the limbo of prehistory, its masterpieces proliferate until, with the modern period, the museum refuses a commitment to current trends and their uncertainties, preferring to wait until time and history make a choice. Always in search of the rare object, the Louvre, in spite of the co-existence of important specialized museums in the Paris region, such as the Guimet or Cernuschi, boasts its own collection of Oriental art. And having the Musée des Arts Décoratifs within its very perimeter makes it possible to juxtapose the décors of life with those masterpieces which history has claimed as the highest achievements of each period. It is a gigantic "complex," as today's term has it, where man's efforts to leave a trace, a legacy upon which his major successes would be inscribed, commingle and complete one another in ever-renewed waves. A gigantic unity where, as we look closely, we see a unity in depth and where, thanks to the close association of what might have been separate museums, and which is now only a rich diversity of "departments," the press of humanity traces its path through the centuries, veering from left to right, but without ever abandoning the common bed-rock from which the tide of man's immense aspiration surges to realize the best within himself. The visitor must pass through numberless galleries in order finally to become aware of that *"élan vital"* of Bergson, of that ardent search whose apparent goals may vary, but which, in its totality, only passes through diverse transformations to reach an exaltation of quality itself—the ultimate rationale of man perhaps—and in any case, his certain attribute.

The museum is pre-eminently an instrument of culture, and culture essentially consists of transcending oneself, to become concerned with what is external to the ego. Since Kant, we have been aware that art was one of the most characteristic expressions of culture, since it is the image of man's most *disinterested* activity. This progressive conquest by which man overcomes his nature and, within the limits of his daily routines, surmounts immediate and direct self-interest, through growing powers of transcendance from animal to man, to reach, finally, that superior degree which we call humanism—these are the stages we can follow through a museum like the Louvre.

Its point of departure was the desire of the Kings of France, a desire nourished by Greed, to establish a collection: and its "seed" may be discerned in its library, so rich in illuminated manuscripts, formed by Charles V in the old Louvre itself, his own palace, which then occupied the southwest corner of the present *Cour Carrée*. With Francis I, we come to the "collector's cabinet," comprising several masterpieces by contemporary Renaissance masters, some of whom were court painters, and foremost of these, Leonardo da Vinci, who died in Francis' castle at Amboise.

The simultaneous acquisition of antique art at this time began to broaden the collection, starting a trend whose peak would be reached under Louis XIV—the study of classical sources and copies of antique culture which dominated the West at that time. Through a policy of individual purchases, combined with the acquisition of international collections already formed by rich private citizens, such as Jabach, the King of France acquired representative objects, landmarks in the development of a civilization upon whose summit he considered himself poised, its progress unfolding from the Age of Pericles to Papal Rome.

Doubt and anxiety appeared in the form of those masterpieces of Venetian art whose political and economic history bridged two different worlds: Central Europe and the northern Germanic world, called "barbaric" by the ancients, and as such, duly ignored, and the East, with Constantinople as its frontier city. From the end of the seventeenth century and the reign of Louis XIV, a new taste began to insinuate itself, one which would entail a change of values and the collapse of old boundaries; a mounting admiration for Northern art, the Dutch and Flemish, whose works would reveal a spirit altogether different from that of the Latins, even while they preached the same lessons.

Thus, those tendencies gathered force which would finally erupt in the nineteenth century, giving birth to Romanticism. France, discovering her solidarity with Northern Europe, tried to lay claim to that area within her own past closest to the contemporary spirit: Medieval art, and especially the Gothic, whose name, however erroneous, was sufficiently indicative of its attraction. The concept of "national antiquities" was exemplified by the Musée des Monuments Français, established during the Revolution, and whose beginnings would soon form the nucleus of the Department of Modern Sculpture in the Louvre. Henceforth, the boundaries of Western culture would be dim; later they would dissolve altogether. Classical Antiquity lost its monopoly on the origins of art, as archeology discovered a territory far more vast. First Egypt, then Mesopotamia, at first known through Assyrian art, revealed those antecedents through which Western art had come into contact with the East. Thanks to French scholars, to their expeditions and excavations, the Louvre could add departments of Egyptology and Assyriology.

Thus the groundwork was laid for the discovery of Oriental civilization, the work of the last half of the nineteenth century: its main impetus was the opening of Japan to foreigners and the ensuing trade which resulted. An important collection of Japanese prints was added to the Drawings Department. It was also at this time that the Louvre yielded to the pressure of still farther reaching curiosity. Interest in so-called primitive societies, Pre-Columbian and African, finally required, at the beginning of the twentieth century, the creation of specialized museums.

In the meantime, another important change had come about. The Royal Collection, gradually opened to visitors, was, in the course of the eighteenth century, transformed into a public museum. The Gallery of Marie de' Medici, painted by Rubens for the Queen Mother's palace in the Luxembourg Gardens (and today in the Louvre) became, under Louis XV, accessible to artists and art lovers at regular visiting hours. It remained for the Revolution to make this change official, by establishing a public Louvre, belonging to the nation and open to all. At this time, it was constituted along the lines of its present organizational structure, and in the nineteenth century several generations of curators were to fill in the outlines of a program of almost world-wide dimensions, but in which the East was still only summarily represented by Islamic art and Japanese prints. The Louvre remains the center of a circle of Parisian museums gravitating around it (it also houses the offices of the Direction of French Museums) which in their totality combine to give a picture of the whole sweep of civilization.

What can we retain from such a vast and complex picture? What guideline is there to follow? Above all else, it is the life spirit of art which we hope to grasp in such a confrontation with time and space. Egypt and Mesopotamia emerge from pre-history, as their societies become organized into agrarian civilizations, whose stability and cumulative revenue made possible the founding of cities, and finally, of the State. In these river valleys, where irrigation is the source of fertility, the primordial problem is one of property: at first, the regulation of agriculture, then the establishment of a system of taxation, the basis of government resources. The primordial science thus became geometry, which organized the division of surfaces and facilitated the re-constitution of fields after flooding.

The most ancient art form serves to evoke religious or historical scenes which constitute a rationale for the image. The problem became one of striking an appropriate balance between respect for the life thus evoked and the simplified order of its depiction. In different, though parallel ways, Egypt and Mesopotamia each resolves this problem in the third century B.C. The scenes of daily life with which artists under the Pharoahs immortalized tomb walls with chisel or brush reveal that same harmony between the perceived and the conceptual that we find in the reliefs of hunting and battle scenes which seventh to ninth century B.C. Assyrian artists carried to their highest point of refinement.

Both civilizations heavily influenced the beginnings of Greek art. Nor should we forget the example provided by the statues of Assyrian Kings. It was Egypt, nonetheless, which first explored the spirit which would reach perfection under Hellenic skies. The Egyptian artist, constrained to repeat subjects fixed and unchangeable in their every detail, was obliged to concentrate all effort, all creative power upon the quality of his work, in the movement of delicacy of the line through which he expressed himself. Thus, to the ordered perfection of form and surface, developed by Greek artists, to the suppleness and freedom allowed them by the birth of the city-state, Egypt was the first to add that subtlety and harmony through which an artist attains the full measure of his powers. Later, at the other end of the earth, Japanese artists would triumph with an equally sublime fusion of craft and spirit.

What was the contribution of Greece? For one, the element of independence. Every citizen was free and thus competed freely within the City. The Greek learned initiative. From more or less perfect imitation, he moved to invention, as much in the objectives of his art (opening a wider area to reality) as in his style (making possible esthetic experiment) and creation. From then on, Greek art was no longer burdened by dogma and tradition, but subject to intellectual examination. The Greek artist questioned art and nature. Conceiving beauty, he forced himself to define it. What had previously been only intuitive, became lucid. Art thus benefited from its new state of consciousness and from the experimentation stimulated by new awareness.

Gradually, Greek art was superseded by Roman, which imitated and copied Greek works, with particular emphasis on their more materialized, naturalistic elements. And, by the same token, the unique aura of quality, the mark of classical genius, evaporated from the Roman copies. Inversely, late Roman art was characterized by a preoccupation with the inner life, which gradually supplanted the search for plastic harmony. The philosophers of the late antique world gave precedence to personal problems of man's destiny, as religion became permeated by currents of mysticism which radically changed its logical structure. Thus the ground was prepared for the seeds of Christianity coming from Judea, in the Eastern Mediterranean. The new faith infiltrated, absorbed and finally overturned the domain of the Roman Empire, replacing the realistic, rational spirit, implanted by Greco-Roman antiquity, with a spiritual fervor, strongly colored by the East. Subsequently, the center of the Western Empire was transferred from Rome to Constantinople, which then became the capital of the Byzantine Empire. For more than ten centuries, the remains of the classical tradition were, in diluted form, absorbed into an art where spiritual realities would henceforth count for more than the realities of the visible world; moreover, this turn towards the East was accentuated by the proximity of Persia, the ancient adversary of Rome, where the last vestiges of Mesopotamian civilization were perpetuated, interwoven with Far Eastern influences carried from China by the route of the silk trade. Such was the new Christian art under the aegis of Byzantium.

The westernmost part of the Mediterranean, however, would remain bound to Europe, and, after the great leveling and vast fusions of the Barbarian invasions, gathered its forces to establish an autonomous Christian civilization which we know as the Middle Ages.

A first Carolingian "Renaissance" in the ninth century tried to bring some coherent order to the surviving elements of antiquity, and acknowledged as valuable sources the contributions of barbarian civilization to areas such as metalwork. In the following century, despite the wave of Eastern influence reinforced first by pilgrimages to the Holy Land, then by the Crusades, the stifled voice of Latin civilization arose with renewed energy. The results of this rebirth was Romanesque art, in which ancient, restored Roman structures were welded to a sculptural repertory in which barbaric elements were joined to those of declining Byzantium and emergent Islam.

But in this opposition of Western civilization reborn and an Eastern world characterized by the Islamic conquest of Byzantium, Europe was the galvanizing force. And this time it was Northern elements, superseding the Latin heritage, which played the more active and creative role. From the beginning of the twelfth century, a new style and spirit predominated, which we call, however inaccurately, Gothic, and whose center was the Ile-de-France. Here the force and vitality, as seen in its architecture and images which turned progressively towards a rediscovery of nature, enveloping the old formalist cult, imbuing it with new intensity and dynamic: the spiritual life of Christianity encountered a source of expression commensurate with its nature.

Soon Europe, under the leadership of an Italy avid to reclaim past glory, would feel equal to the task of rebinding herself to the tradition of classical antiquity and to revive within this new civilization the spirit which had forged the ancient grandeur of the West. Painting emerged and asserted itself in the course of the declining Middle Ages; its role then had been a modest one, limited to miniatures and to a few frescoes. The dominant religion had enlisted the best talents in a campaign for the beautification of its churches. And there, the art of mosaic, Byzantine in origin and translated to Italy, of stained glass, the magical development of a barbarian art, and, again, of tapestry, were, in the North, subsidiary to architecture. The devout were absorbed by a common faith and preferred those arts better adapted to a collective scale. Then, with the thirteenth century, the rise of the bourgeoisie gave new directions to art; with hard-won material wealth, and the sense of personal property, art returned to a worldly and human level. The painting, property or gift of a corporation, was soon to become more and more often a private possession, the pride and delight of its owner, and thus assumed a growing importance. And with this change, painting began to reign supreme.

In the fourteenth and fifteenth centuries, however, Italy and the Northern countries manifested these changes differently. Medieval Italy was dominated by Byzantine influences, which had carried the spiritual inspiration and ascetic aspects of Christianity to their highest degree. Mosaics, schematic and sanctified with their shimmering gold backgrounds, suggested the approach of the divinity. Italian painting thus had the task of placing these theological abstractions within reality, returning these schema to a world of volumes and space. Naturally, this new art sought the positive forms which it needed to reincarnate them from the still-viable traditions of Greco-Roman sculpture. From the spiritualized abstractions of Byzantium, Italian art moved uninterruptedly towards those structures which reason brilliantly conceived and then generalized. The Virgin of Cimabue indicates the brilliance with which this transition was accomplished. Like Giotto in the next generation, these artists had not abandoned a world dominated by the intellect; they simply modified the concepts of theocentric transcendance with more rational evidence.

In the Northern countries, the other pole of European art, this departure created special problems: their artists had also been formed by a Middle Ages bathed in Christian fervor, in which every attribute of the visible world was a symbol of God. But here, more than elsewhere, and particularly in the Low Countries, where the cloth-trade played a dominant economic role, material realities had imparted to faith a more concrete consistency, very close to the things of this world and their presence. Since the thirteenth century, the Middle Ages had inclined towards a growing realism. One might say that throughout the Western world, a natural movement of gravity led from the divine to the human level, but in Northern Europe, this movement was conceived as a vindication of the senses and of external observation. Italy, however, nourished by the sense of her antique past as the highest point of civilization, saw in the Renaissance the occasion to revive pagan culture (as witness, for example, the *Parnassus* of Mantegna, or the *Apollo and Marsyas* of Perugino) and interpreted this movement on an intellectual plane, as a flowering of intelligence in all its forms.

The Flemish found their mode of expression at the beginning of the fifteenth century with the art of Jan van Eyck and his new discoveries in oil technique, which made possible an illusionist rendering of the material aspect of the universe. At the beginning of the sixteenth century, Quentin Metsys demonstrates, in *Portrait of a Moneychanger and his Wife,* how quickly the evolution had taken place; brilliant rendering is placed at the service of a concrete vision and specific interest. The way was opened for Dutch naturalism of the seventeenth century and the subtle, rigorous recording of everyday existence. The genius alone could occasionally assert the individual spark of his own sensibility, to transform the flatness of reality by the crystalline purity of the soul which perceived it: such an artist was Jan Vermeer of Delft.

When Italy turned to the same problems of transcribing the visual world, she interpreted their solution less as a tribute to the powers of vision than as an exaltation of those of intelligence, capable of solving problems in every domain. For it was intellect which organized and constructed the forms designed to render volume, intellect which organized and constructed perspective, devised to translate the breadth and depth of space wherein these volumes would be placed. In Italian painting as well, geometric analysis often took precedence over optical analysis, as seen, for example, in the fifteenth-century *Rout of San Romano* of Paolo Uccello. This rigor, the basis for Leonardo Da Vinci's observation that painting is a "cosa mentale" was nonetheless tempered by two factors: one, inherited from the near medieval past was the continuation of that moving tenderness of divine revelation, disseminated by the Gothic influence and present to a greater degree in Sienese art whose more emotive genius found its most typical expression in Simone Martini than in Florentine painting, where genius assumed more intellectual form, exemplified by the art of Ghirlandaio whose charm is invested with intense fervor. The other factor was the inevitable influence of Northern painting, whose scientific technique Italian artists, like Antonello da Messina and Giovanni Bellini (Mantegna's brother-in-law) were proud to have acquired for their own.

Thus the way was prepared for that great flowering of Italian art which took place in the sixteenth century, the High Renaissance. Italian artists joined the sources of optics, developed by the North, to the intellectual organization unique to their own tradition. Yet at the same time, this art retained the sense of transcendance which, reaching towards God in past centuries, now tended towards a more worldly interpretation: the search for quality as expressed by an ideal of beauty.

In the works of three great masters, these elements are fused and carried to their culminating point of genius. The eldest was Leonardo da Vinci, whose youth was formed by the fifteenth century, and in whose art all the possibilities of painting were subjected to the domination of the human mind, conscious and proud of its powers, daring even to extend them to that farthest realm where only intuition and the unconscious were thought to reside. The *Mona Lisa* penetrates the enigma of being, respected in all its indefinable nature. Leonardo still stirs the shadowy regions, expressive of his magic. Raphael, on the other hand, makes the purest light unequivocally reveal the harmonies of body and soul. His *Portrait of Baldassare Castiglione* is the quintessential humanist. But with the art of the third giant, Michelangelo, we already hear the rumblings of discontent, a need to burst every limitation, as we can see in his *Slave*, strangled by his crushing burden. The unquenchable yearning of the Baroque, soon to supersede Classicism throughout Europe and to rekindle the stormy passions of life, was already beginning to emerge.

A closer link between Northern and Mediterranean Europe was created, at this same period, by Venetian painting, the northernmost school of Italian art. Imbued more than the others by the spirit of the East, Venice, whose seaport led to the Orient, was also an outlet for the Germanic countries. Dürer, the greatest German painter of the Renaissance, made several long visits there. Like Flanders, with whom it enjoyed close relations, Venice was ruled by a mercantile patrician class. It was Venetian artists who shattered the boundaries of Italian genius, with its tendency to be limited by pure intelligence. Here, conversely, an insatiable taste developed for material splendors—the richness of flesh, fabrics, color and light. But where the North had taught them to copy with veracity, Venice, having once absorbed this fifteenth-century lesson, transformed it by means of such opulent additions to the painting itself as colored glass inlays. Among the great High Renaissance painters, it was Corregio of Parma who could most subtly evoke this shiver of sensuality. From Giorgione, who died prematurely, to his friend Titian, who dominated the century, to Veronese, inventor of tonal harmonies hitherto unimagined in their coloristic brilliance and silvery sheen, to Tintoretto, whose frustrated and tormented genius seems to usher in the age of modern anxiety—these painters all revealed an art whose repercussions would be enormous for the destiny of painting: henceforth, painting would have to discover within itself those riches which previously it had been content to transcribe. And no painter exemplifies this discovery with as much coloristic subtlety and technical daring as Velazquez.

Venice, however, had still other contributions to make. From the very beginning of the sixteenth century, Giorgione had shown that art could be the most secretive, as well as most profound expression of the artist's personality, and the orchestration of colors and light could, as in music, be the emanations of a soul. His *Concert Champêtre* reveals a universe born of the artist's dreams, to which he has given himself and through which he appears to others. Somewhat later than Giorgione, a more solitary and bitter genius, El Greco, moving from Greece to Venice before settling in Spain, created works of such violently personal vision that for a long time they were considered merely bizarre and ignored as such.

It was only with the seventeenth century that these newly liberated forces were to reveal all their potential. In Italy, at the very start of the century, Caravaggio abruptly broke with the Renaissance ideal of formal beauty. Thus the way was paved for a new art form: in Flanders, Rubens substituted the flood of life in all its lyricism for the scientific harmony of form, in that same Baroque direction begun by Michelangelo; in Holland, Frans Hals expressed this verve with a technique so boldly modern as to surpass the Venetians in its freedom; here, too, Rembrandt exhausting every resource of personal vision, revealed what a powerful and profound nature could leave the world through its own imprint—a breadth and significance which shattered and eclipsed the literal sense of vision. Reworked, recreated, this vision became nothing less than the soul made manifest in all its unknown power to discover in the depths of itself that spiritual retreat which it had sought since the Middle Ages within a communal faith, and for which the Renaissance had substituted the organization of intellectual and positive resources of tangible reality.

Thus each school of European painting had its turn at the center of the stage as, in turn, the contribution of each became more highly evolved. Until this time, French painting had played more of a mediating role. Midway between Italy and the North, French art had, during the Middle Ages and the reign of the Gothic, dominated the Northern regions of Europe; its "primitive" painters were more allied to the Flemish esthetic, while bringing to this tradition their own qualities of delicacy and tenderness. In the south, however, French painting displayed its particular aptitude to participate in the Mediterranean genius, as we can see in the almost Spanish accents of the Avignon *Pietà*.

The French vocation for-psychology may be seen in the work of a brilliant series of portraitists. Fouquet, formed by the traditions of Italy where he had studied, was the most highly representative in the fifteenth century. In the sixteenth, affinities with Northern realism became, especially with Clouet, more sharply defined. From then on, the intermediate position of France allowed her to turn to the growing prestige of the Italian High Renaissance for lessons in harmony, to which, with the School of Fontainebleau, France added the pronounced elegance of her own tradition. This appropriation of classical territory became still more defined in the seventeenth century when the two greatest French painters, Poussin and Claude Lorrain settled in Rome. That spiritual realism, however, in which the national equilibrium found its expression, was represented by the Le Nain brothers, by Georges de La Tour (influenced by Caravaggio and only recently discovered) and by French still-life painting.

In the seventeenth century, a change in direction made it possible for French painting, threatened by desiccation, to turn towards Rubens and to Flemish art, finding, so to speak, an antidote in the life and lyricism of the North. Boucher confined himself to conferring a new sensual vitality upon a classical repertory, but his disciple, Fragonard, with more audacity still, borrowed as much from Rubens as from Rembrandt. And the painting of Chardin brings together all the resources of a newly liberated pictorial craft applied to the traditions of familiar realism.

Nonetheless France, now moving to the cultural forefront, whose influence spread increasingly throughout Europe, was still to make her major contribution to Western art. Her psychological vocation, ever more refined, was the genesis of the marvel which is French portraiture, whether painting or sculpture. Through it, she would achieve the perfect fusion of two recent revelations which had shaken European art: this vocation consciously sought to express the individual in those areas which seemed to defy revelation, and to this end, it forged a language whose pictorial technique created a new domain. From the very beginning of the eighteenth century, and even before the death of Louis XIV, Watteau had revealed himself, in this double role, to be an innovator as astounding as had been Giorgione, his predecessor by two centuries. Watteau's example was not to be understood immediately. The nineteenth century, on the contrary, began by the attempt to revive the classical disciplines, as exemplified by the art of David and his disciple, Ingres. Baron Gros provided a counter-current to this Neo-Classicism, and finally, Géricault galvanized these spiritual outpourings and Romanticism reached its plenitude. Another painter, Delacroix, united classical reflection with Romantic passion to nourish a lyric power illuminating an ardent soul consumed by torment and yearning, at the same time that this painter's interest in the exotic breached the boundaries of traditional culture.

Delacroix's art was superseded by Realism which leaned heavily upon scientific discoveries and a triumphant positivism. From Millet's epic vision to the substantial Courbet, this movement reassured itself, through a patient observation of reality, that it was doomed. The Impressionists, whose goal had been to extend Realism, ended by exhausting it. The role of energy, that particular element of contemporary life, was just then revealed to them, exciting their interest in its most visible expression —light. In the mid-nineteenth century, Corot became the most delicate bard of light, reflecting the exquisite and dreamy sensibility incarnate in his figures and landscapes. Under the impetus of Corot, the Impressionists sacrificed everything to the investigation of light first begun by Claude Lorrain. Degas was followed by Toulouse-Lautrec who, resisting this trend, continued to explore the possibilities of realism by consecrating it to the observation of contemporary life, and by endowing this realism with the mordancy which gives his art its particularly modern stamp. Change had also come about with Manet, an older painter, who both transformed Impressionism and was influenced by it, while, at the same time, remaining faithful to a classical construction of space. In the following generation, Camille Pissarro still retained a rustic density inherited from Millet. It was, however, Claude Monet, above all, who atomized the universe, hurling it into a chromatic vibration in which form and matter were definitively dissolved. From then on, the real had lost its reality: the traditional scaffolding of painting had collapsed.

Consequently, painting now had to be reconstructed. Renoir, already allied to tradition through his admiration for Rubens and Delacroix, remained faithful to the carnal architecture of the body and exalted it. The Post-Impressionists, led by Paul Cézanne, while yielding nothing of the Impressionists' optical veracity, returned painting to its pure elements: form and color, and by expressing one through the other, proved each to possess a unique force distinct from imitation. From this revelation were to emerge Cubism and abstract art. Gauguin's contribution carried him a step further, proving that form and color could be used in all combinations, thus breaking the shackles of truth, as measured by the familiar appearance of things, and devoting his art, instead, to expressive force, to reveal the inner world of the artist. His contemporary, van Gogh forged ahead in this same direction, casting colors and forms into a burning brazier where, flaming and twisting, their fire illuminated the tormented bursts of the artist's sensibility.

Everything was ready for a new era in art, an era in which the artist would have the freedom to find grandeur outside of his own past and his own traditions.

# ANCIENT EGYPT

SEATED SCRIBE. *V Dynasty.*

This famous statue of an unnamed scribe was discovered in the course of a disorganized excavation conducted by the famous 19th-century French Egyptologist Auguste Edouard Mariette at Sakkara. In 1921, it was found to bear a close resemblance to a seated statue of the monarch Kai which had been shipped to the Louvre after the same excavation. This Egyptian official has thus survived in two monuments.

The statue is considered one of the masterpieces of Egyptian art. On the one hand it is intensely realistic, particularly in the level gaze of the eyes, which are inlaid with highly polished hard stone. On the other hand, and in striking contrast to this realism, the sculptural forms are severely geometric. The figure is adamantly frontal, preserving something of the original four-sided block of stone from which it was cut. It is as if the artist had thought in terms of four juxtaposed bas-reliefs instead of a monument in the round. This peculiarly Egyptian attitude toward the block leaves its traces in almost all Egyptian sculpture, and is evident, for example, in the flat planes of the scribe's back.

Egyptian art is characterized by the artists' attempts to seek out and depict a figure's most typical or most significant view. Hence we find profile heads with eyes shown frontally, and frontal torsos with legs and arms in profile. This approach is connected with man's normal vision and is always present to a greater or lesser extent in primitive arts. Yet one cannot call Egyptian art "primitive." It is with civilizations of the ancient periods that certain rules for principal views (in painting and for reliefs) and for frontality (in sculpture in the round) become binding. These two aspects stem from one and the same phenomenon, based on a new need for architectonic order and pictographic clarity. The mastabas and pyramids of Old Kingdom Egypt expressed this need for geometric and architectonic order, while the development of hieroglyphic writing did the same for pictographic, narrative clarity. From then on, the canon affected every branch of Egyptian art, its repertory lasting for millennia. The sculptor of the V dynasty, however, while working in a tradition which was already centuries old, was not subdued completely by the system. He accepted parts of the code, but he felt free enough to make a few choices on his own, filling out a given scheme with his own esthetic experience. Thus he was able to add realist touches to the otherwise abstract figure of the Seated Scribe.

*Seated Scribe*
V Dynasty (2563–2423 B.C.):
circa 2500 B.C.
Painted limestone; 21″ high
From Sakkara.

HEAD OF KING DEDEFRE. *IV Dynasty.*

King Dedefre's portrait, while as realistic as the representations of courtiers in the Old Kingdom, differs from them in its smooth, firm

modeling. His royal crown *(nemsit),* with the emblematic snake *(ureus)* rising above the headband, imparts a Cubistic quality to the head with a suggestion of architectonic modules.

*Above:*

*Head of a Young Man*
IV Dynasty (2723–2563 B.C.) or Amarnian period (second quarter of XIV century B.C.) Painted limestone; 13 1/4″ high. Origin unknown; formerly in the Salt collection, thus known as the "Salt Head."

*Left:*

*Head of King Dedefre, Cheop's Brother and Immediate Successor*
IV Dynasty; XXVII century B.C.
Red Sandstone; 11″ high
From Aburoash.

HEAD OF A YOUNG MAN (THE SALT HEAD). *IV Dynasty (?).* The so-called Salt Head—named after its former owner—has been dated to periods as much as 14 centuries apart, a startling difference of opinion which is explicable only in the case of an art like Egypt's, where the artistic language crystallized at the dawn of its history and remained uninflected by the passing of the centuries. This head is problematic because of its relative independence of the Egyptian esthetic code. It has a naturalism characteristic of just two phases in Egyptian art—the Old Kingdom, with its nascent realism, and the Amarna phase, with its markedly realistic trend. The Salt Head seems to fit better into the second of the two because of its "life-mask" quality typical of certain works from the Amarna epoch.

GIRL WITH A LOTUS. *V Dynasty (?).*
This representation of a girl smelling a flower exemplifies the technique

*Girl with Lotus*
V Dynasty (?)
Painted limestone; 21″ high.

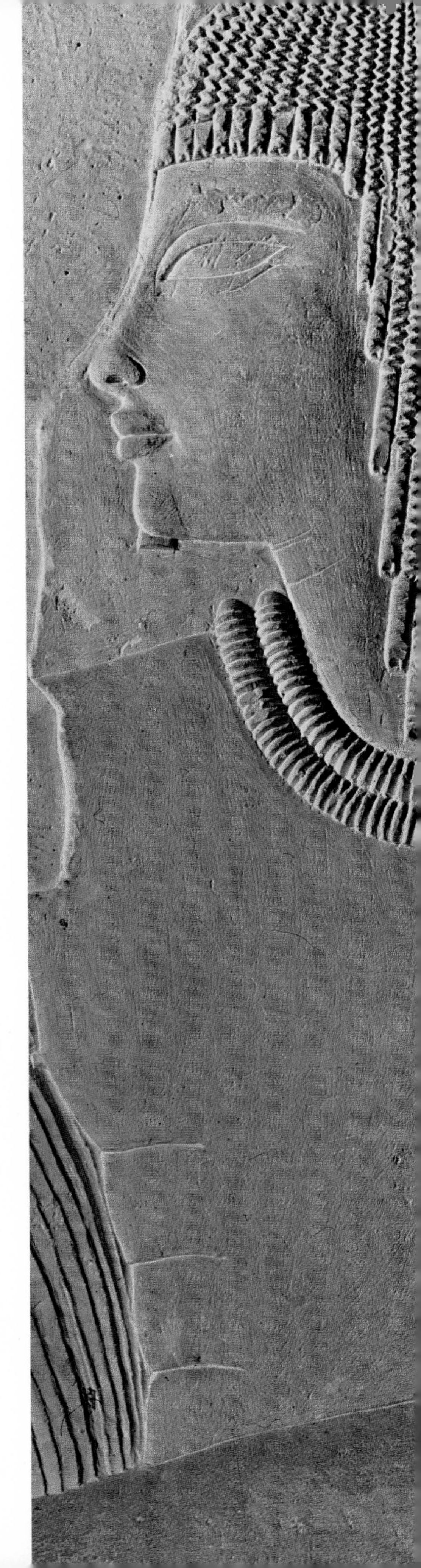

*Amenmes and His Wife*
End of XVIII Dynasty
Detail of funerary relief.
Limestone; 21 3/5″ × 25 3/5″.

*Reherka and Mersankh*
V Dynasty
Detail of a family group.
Painted limestone; 20 4/5″ high.

of incised relief work, a favorite medium in Egyptian art. Rather than projecting from the background, the body receives the dimension of depth only by the incision of its outlines. This gives the figure an abstract quality akin to the effect achieved by modern solar photography and emphasizes the contour lines, which assume a fluid elegance almost independent of the body.

REHERKA AND MERSANKH. *V Dynasty.*
A characteristic Old Kingdom type of statue is the family group, in which the figures were conceived as separate entities and juxtaposed. There is also the "false" group, in which two statues representing the same person are paired. In the latter, the image has become a definitive symbol: no longer are two "objects" occupying the same space, but an idea is repeated twice within the same context. The group Raherka and Mersankh, on the other hand, is distinguished by a more explicit intention to represent reality by giving the pair a more naturalistic appearance, with the woman leaning confidently on the man.

AMENMES AND HIS WIFE. *XVIII Dynasty.*
Amenmes' funerary relief, datable around the Amarna period, typifies the Theban school in the New Kingdom. The stylistic conventions clearly belong to the code developed in the Old and Middle Kingdoms, yet they are confined here by a discipline which was previously absent.

*Pharaoh Taharka Offering Two Wine Cups to the Falcon God Hemen*
XXV "Ethiopian" Dynasty (circa 689–680 B.C.) Schist, wood, bronze (the base is covered with silver, the falcon is gilded); 7 4/5″ high, 4″ wide, 10 1/4″ long.

The originality of the work lies in the subtle variations on the traditional rhythmic composition and design. Here, as in the relief of the Girl with a Lotus, we can appreciate the elegance of the outline and the clarity of incision.

THE PHAROAH TAHARKA OFFERING TWO WINE CUPS TO THE FALCON GOD HEMEN. *XXV Dynasty.*
Bronze sculpture which flourished in Mesopotamia, appears later in Egypt than elsewhere in the Near East. Small bronzes are common in Egypt only after the XXII Dynasty, and are often inlaid with precious metals or decorated with gold leaf.

PREPARATIONS FOR A BANQUET. *V Dynasty.*
The detail illustrated here comes from a series of reliefs which decorated the walls of the funerary chapel of the Mastaba of Akhuthotep. Banquet scenes like this were conventional in Egyptian funerary art, and they served to project earthly pleasures into the afterlife. Apparently Akhuthotep died before the decoration of his chapel was finished. The registers above the portion illustrated here still bear traces of squared-off guidelines which served either as a guide for enlarging a smaller drawing of the banquet scene or as modules for an artist working with canonical proportions. Either possibility demonstrates the academism of pharaonic art, which, more than in any other art, tied artists to traditions established by the past. Yet at the same time Egyptian art was not static. To the casual observer there may be no difference between this work and that of the New Kingdom, but closer examination of this relief compared to that of Amenmes is instructive. Two butchers grasp the leg of an ox and one of them slices it with a large knife. Their torsos are shown in profile from the shoulder down, while Amenmes' torso is shown frontally; at the same time the legs and heads of all three are in profile. The attempt to show the butchers in complete profile heightens the strong diagonals of the composition, which combine with the rectilinear forms of the bodies and the curves of the animal's leg to create a subtle interplay of linear motifs and triangular spaces.

*Preparations for a Banquet*
Detail from reliefs in the funerary chapel of the Mastaba of Akhuthotep
V Dynasty
Painted limestone; 14″ high.

ROYAL HEAD. *XVIII Dynasty.*
A typical product of the Amarna period, this wooden head decorated the top of a harp. The styles characteristic of this period were connected with the religious reforms of Amenhotep IV—Ikhnaton. The term "expressionistic" has often been applied to the monuments of this period because of their curious combination of realistic with stylized linear elements. The head illustrated here resembles official portraits of the Pharaoh, whose physical abnormality may have formed the basis for the experimental stylization typical of the Amarna period. It is the product of a refined art, with its delicate interplay of soft curves and long smooth planes, expressing something akin to the European decorations of the late nineteenth-century Art Nouveau period.

*Above:*

*Royal Head*
End of XVIII Dynasty
Opaque two-toned glass (formerly inlaid with stone and metal); 3 1/2″ high.

ROYAL HEAD. *XVIII Dynasty.*
This head of a young Pharaoh is covered with two glazes of blue faience. If, as is probable, this is a head of Tutenkhamon, it would be one of the most typically Amarnian works of his brief reign. Especially characteristic is the oblique slant of the enormous almond eyes, which, as in the art of the Extreme Orient, is more a stylistic than a racial trait, its source lying in a keen feeling for the sophistications of linear design.

*Left:*

*Royal Head*
End of XVIII Dynasty
Ornament in colored wood for top of a harp (formerly inlaid with stone and metal in the eye sockets and eyebrows); height of entire piece 7 1/4″ of which about 3″ were inserted in the neck of the instrument. From Tell el Amarna; acquired by the Louvre in 1932.

SPHINX FROM TANIS. *Middle Kingdom.*
The Hyksos king Apopi, Meneptah (son of Rameses II), and Seshonk I (XXII Dynasty) in turn usurped the colossal Sphinx of Tanis which dates from the Middle Kingdom (reigns of Sesotri III and Amenemhet III) as well as other examples from the same era. Ancient as this stone representation is, the iconography of the sphinx is even older.

*Sphinx from Tanis*
Middle Kingdom
Red granite; 81″ high, 136″ long.

OSTRAKON: RAMESSIDE HEAD WITH THE ATTRIBUTES OF OSIRIS. *XX Dynasty.*

The Greek work *ostraka* (meaning sherd or shell) is used to designate stone scraps or fragments on which Egyptian artists made sketches of preparatory designs, and these have been found in relatively large numbers. They probably were studies for paintings, rather than sculpture, as the summary indications of color suggest. In general these sketches are merely outlines, similar to those traced on walls preceding the execution of stone reliefs.

The drawing illustrated here demonstrates the characteristic graphic mannerism of the XIX Dynasty, the origin of which might be connected with the linearism of Amarnian art. The nose has the characteristic curving profile and the eye is reduced to an elegant ornamental motif. It is no longer schematic, as the Egyptian canon demanded, but hints at a more naturalistic profile.

THE SINGER OF AMON, ZEDKHONSUAUFANKH, PLAYS THE HARP BEFORE THE GOD HARMAKHIS. *New Kingdom.*

The singer, on his knees before the seated figure of the god, plays a harp decorated with a royal head. The man's face is depicted in the expressionistic manner of the Amarna period, both in the interplay of curve and plane and in the realistic feature of the open mouth holding its note for all eternity. The colors are elementary—a white background, with areas of red-orange, dark green and yellow—but the brushwork is fluid and easy, so that the outlines and the bodies they define blend into a whole.

*The Singer of Amon, Zedkhonsuaufankh, Plays the Harp before the God Harmakhis*
New Kingdom
Painted wood; 11 1/2″ high.

*Ostrakon: Ramesside Head with the Attributes of Osiris*
XX Dynasty (1200–1085 B.C.)
Sketch in red and black for a wall decoration;
limestone; 8 1/3″ high.

*Statue of the Chancellor Nakht*
Middle Kingdom, XII Dynasty
(1991–1786 B.C.)
Painted wood (inlaid eyes); 69″ high.
From Assiut.



STATUE OF THE CHANCELLOR NAKHT. *XII Dynasty.*
The statue of Nakht is one of the most remarkable pieces of wooden sculpture preserved from the Middle Kingdom. It retains traces of original polychromy and is almost completely covered by red paint. The rigid frontality of the figure follows the tradition of Old Kingdom sculpture. In comparison with Memphis statuary, this statue demonstrates a tighter synthesis of volumes, avoiding any unnecessary deviation from pure geometric forms. Thus the roundness of the head is accentuated by its smoothness (hair was probably painted on), and the nose has no nostrils. Similarly, the long skirt with its stiff apron forms a truncated pyramid and reflects an architectural feeling for geometric form. The arms hang stiffly at the sides of the body, yet the artist has injected a certain naturalism in the gesture of the right hand, which pulls the garment aside hiding the thumb in a crease of the cloth.

TORSO OF ISIS. *Ptolemaic Period.*
The torso is undoubtedly a fragment of a statue of Isis. The frontality of the figure, left leg advancing slightly, the stiffly hanging arms, the round breasts and the exaggerated height of the stomach are entirely in keeping with the Egyptian artistic tradition. Yet if one compares this work with a torso from the Amarna period, the influence of Greek art becomes evident. The drapery, knotted below the breasts and falling down the body between the legs, is depicted with a certain plasticity not apparent in the Amarna torso, where the lines are incised rather than modeled. This statue is not, however, a product of a colonial art, nor is it a Greek version of a traditional Egyptian work, a copy done by someone with antiquarian interests. It is a product of an indigenous culture which was becoming increasingly Hellenized in spite of a desire to remain faithful to Egyptian tradition.

FEMALE TORSO. *XVIII Dynasty.*
The fragment illustrated here is typical of the Amarna style, not as much for the linear quality of the drapery as for the prominent stomach and thighs. The former motif goes back to the dawn of Egyptian art, and in the course of the XVIII Dynasty found wide expression and numerous modifications. The latter shows an attempt to project horizontal and vertical lines into a third dimension, rounding the surface of the relief as if it were a portion of the body of a vase. This feature also characterizes pharaonic iconography, and its source has been sought in the supposed physical deformation of Ikhnaton. It could lie, however, in the artists' deliberate rebellion against the traditionally contained, almost columnar forms of Egyptian art; the result of this rebellion found an analogy in the ideal of the "pregnant nude," which also characterized European art in the late Gothic period.

*Torso of Isis*
Ptolemaic Period (Greek-Alexandrian)
330–30 B.C.
Diorite sculpture in the round; 27 1/4″ high.

*Female Torso*
End of XVIII Dynasty (1370–60 B.C.)
Red quartz; 11 4/5″ high.
Probably from Tell el Amarna

HEAD OF A PRINCESS. *XVIII Dynasty.*
The extraordinary refinement and surprising versatility of the Amarna period attains full expression in this fragment found in Tell el Amara, dating from the end of Ikhnaton's revolution (more precisely, between the reigns of Ikhnaton and Tutenkhamon, 1358 B.C.). The asymmetry of the wig, apparently characteristic of children's hair fashions, stands in contrast to the symmetry and geometric precision of the face. The cheeks seem as if traced out by a compass, and the hairline forms the third side of an equilateral triangle with curved sides. The curve of the chin is echoed by the curve of the lips, and the arching eyesockets repeat the flare of the nostrils. Thus the artist in his own way has reaffirmed the Egyptian principles of reducing human features to an esthetic formula.

SARCOPHAGUS OF DJEDKHONSOUIOUFANKH. *XXVI Dynasty.*
The most ancient mummies had faces painted on the wrappings around the deceased persons' heads. Later the sarcophagus itself, like the wrappings, was given the form of the mummy and painted with human features. Often the mummy was contained in multiple sarcophagi, each one shaped like the body and painted. Wooden anthropomorphic sarcophagi generally date no earlier than the New Kingdom. The painted decoration is always religious in character, depicting the soul's voyage to the afterlife and the deities it will meet, as well as the judgment to which it must submit. The Egyptians also wrote various exorcisms and entire chapters of *The Book of the Dead* are devoted to sarcophagi. Apart from their religious significance, they are extraordinary artistic creations, their anthropomorphic character abstracted and reduced to an elegant stylization. The mummy became an idol, covered with a lively polychrome decoration executed by an artist with a sure sense of composition and a profound understanding of the medium he was using.

NECKLACE OF THE PHARAOH PINEDJEM. *XXI Dynasty.*
Egyptian artists took pleasure in ornamental design for its own sake, and consequently they found jewelry a most satisfactory medium for expression. The jewelry of the New Kingdom, which includes the famous treasure of Tutenkhamon, excels in its refinement, technical precision and thoughtful juxtaposition of enamel, precious stones and gold. Pinedjem's necklace demonstrates the high level of workmanship in the exquisitely fine links of the triple chain, the elegant pendants and the plaque decorated with a sacred scarab crowned by the solar disk.

*Head of a Princess*
End of XVIII Dynasty
Limestone; 6″ high.
From Tell el Amarna.

*Sarcophagus of Djedkhonsouioufankh*
XXVI Dynasty (circa 660–525 B.C.)
Mummy cover. Sculptured wood, stucco and polychrome; 63″ long.

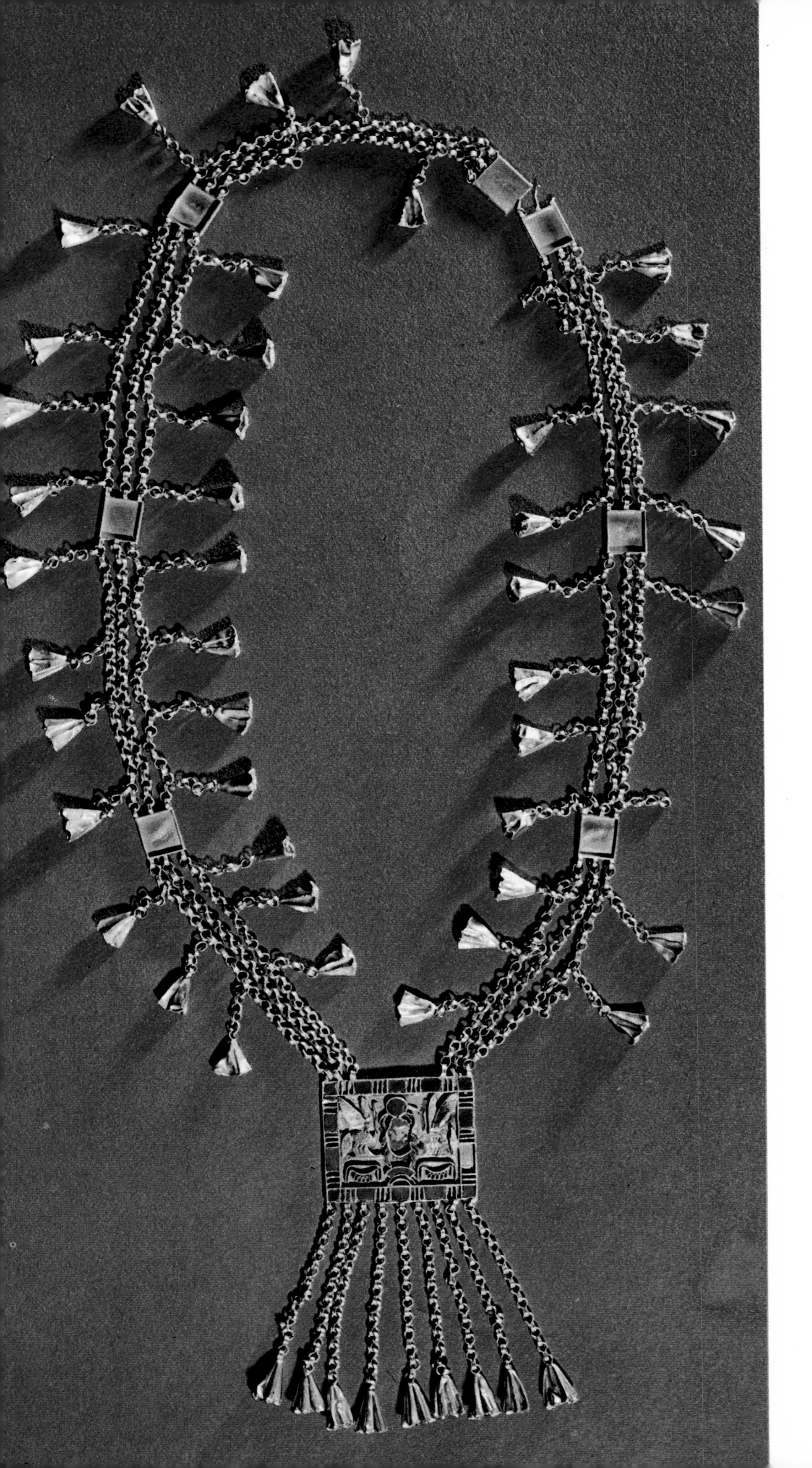

*Necklace of the Pharaoh Pinedjem*
End of New Kingdom, Thebes, XXI Dynasty; circa 1030 B.C.
Necklace with flower-shaped pendants and rectangular centerpiece. Gold and silver and lapis lazuli; 19 3/5″ long.

# ASIA MINOR

*Goddess of Fertility*
Second half of Third Millennium B.C.
Terra-cotta placque with red varnish;
25" high. From Cyprus.

GODDESS OF FERTILITY. *Third Millennium B.C.*
During the Bronze Age, Cyprus was inhabited by a civilization closely related to the contemporary cultures of the Anatolian coast and the region of Syria, and at the same time profited from certain links with the Aegean. This island civilization produced the little goddess illustrated here, one of the oldest examples of a class characterized by the geometric stylization of the human figure. Only the ears and the tip of the nose project from the flat rectangular stone surface. The borders of the garment, the necklaces and arms are indicated by simple incision, while the eyes, nostrils, the mouth, the hands and the "pearls" of the necklaces are indicated by small holes punched in the surface. The idol is the expression of an abstract style, the result of a considered rather than casual composition, stemming from the magic and arcane symbolism of a prehistoric civilization. The contemporary Surrealist Max Ernst, in his recent *Ubu Father and Son,* probably had in mind this kind of idol and the impressiveness of its magical abstraction.

STELE OF NARAMSU'EN. *End of the Third Millennium B.C.*
The Akkadians ruled Mesopotamia without seriously disrupting Sumerian culture during the two centuries between the Proto-Dynastic and the Late Sumerian periods. Akkadian sculptors, however, when faced with the heavy, rough figure style of the older civilization (which did influence them at times) and the stiff formality of its representations in relief, proved themselves closer, more attentive observers of nature than were their Sumerian counterparts. The Stele of Naramsu'en is an exceptional monument, and is probably the oldest work of art we know in which the artist attempted to represent the idea of space. He clearly intended to show a natural, realistic relationship between the human figures and their topographical setting rather than succumbing to a traditional stylization. His task was rendered easier in part by the conformation of the place represented, a mountainside; and by the scene shown, an assault by the Akkadians on a hill tribe. The foothills appear as undulating lines building up to the mountain peak. Thus the sculptor had an excuse for showing one figure on top of the other. In a normal representation of a crowd standing in a flat area, artists traditionally projected the idea of several rows of people using this same disposition, without the visual rationale of a sloping terrain. Similarly, the sculptor gave a certain movement to the background by placing various warriors on successively higher foothills. He indicates that the higher a person is the farther away he is from the viewer by showing him behind someone on a foothill lower in the relief. The sculptor has not yet reached the point of showing that mountains and hills can hide or half-hide human figures. For this sophistication, one must wait another 19 centuries until the appearance of the Argonaut Krater (also in the Louvre).

*Stele of the Victory of Naramsu'en, King of Akkad*
Sippar: period of Akkadian Rule; phase III, circa 2389–2353 B.C. Pink sandstone; 78 4/5″ high, 41 1/3″ wide. Commemorative stele from Susa; taken as war plunder in XII century B.C. by King Shutruknahhunte, after the Babylonian conquest of Sippar and other cities.

## THE PRIEST ABIHIL OF THE TEMPLE OF ISHTAR.

*Third Millennium B.C.*

The bearded and bald Abihil wears the sheepskin skirt typical of the Sumerians in this period. He sits on a wicker stool, his hands clasped in prayer. The small size of the statue, its compactness and geometric rotundity is typical of the Proto-Dynastic epoch, and more particularly of the Fara period, of which this is one of the finest works known. Also characteristic are the large eyes, rendered intense and piercing by the inlaid colored stone. Although this statue is conceived frontally, it seems less rigidly confined by its four-sided approach than the Seated Scribe from Egypt. The curves and planes of the body are rounded off, giving the figure a rotund appearance, disguising the fact that, as in Egypt, the artist thinks in terms of two-dimensional surfaces joined together to create a third dimension.

*The Priest Abihil of the Temple of Ishtar at Mari*
Predynastic epoch, Fara phase (ancient Shurupak in Sumer): circa 2900–2685 (?) B.C. Detail of seated figure. Alabaster with bitumen inlays (eyebrows) and lapis lazuli (eyes); 20 3/5" high. From Mari, now called Tell-Hariri on the Euphrates.

## VOTIVE TABLET OF URNANSHE. *III Millennium B.C.*

In this Sumerian votive tablet, the ruler Urnanshe is depicted twice, each time followed by the diminutive figure of a servant. In the upper register, he carries a basket on his head filled with materials for the construction of a temple; in the lower, he is shown seated on a throne. Before him stand his numerous children, four above and four below, identified by their respective names. It is not clear who is the personage of larger size preceding the children in the upper row, whether a first-born who died before the father (the latter was in fact succeeded by Akurgal, shown in second position), a daughter or a priestess. The figures are reduced to mere stereotypes, designed according to the conventions of combining front and side views, and scaled according to rank. This is more like pictograph or picture writing than figurative art. The intention is clearly utilitarian and informative; little attention is given to even the most elementary requirements of composition, and writings fill the voids in disorderly fashion, even covering the figures themselves.

*Votive Tablet of Urnanshe*
Sumeric art of the predynastic epoch
Ur I phase: circa 2630 B.C.
Limestone; 15 3/5" high, 18 1/2" wide.
From Tello (ancient Girsu).

*Gudea*
High-dynastic epoch, period of late Sumerian princedoms, Gudea phase (circa 2290–2255 B.C.) Statuette without inscriptions. Diorite, 41 1/3″ high. From Lagash; to the Louvre in 1953.

GUDEA. *Third Millennium B.C.*
Late Sumerian sculpture continued along the same lines followed in the Akkadian period, except that historical reliefs disappear from the scene. There are numerous statues of pious local nobles and princes in the act of praying. Gudea alone dedicated some thirty monuments. The well-dressed Sumerian here wears a large mantle with a fringed border and a cap which appears to be of lambskin. The figure is still frontal, with a stylized rotundity accented by the smooth surface of the drapery. This last feature may result from the artist's confrontation with an especially hard stone (diorite) or from some Egyptian influence. The proportions of the figure are typically Sumerian, in the compact solidity of the body and in the comparatively large head, hands and feet. Like the priest Abihil, the eyes are unnaturally large, and although the inlay is now missing, at one time he, too, had the singularly intense stare so characteristic of the Sumerian style.

VASE FROM SUSA. *Circa 2000 B.C.*
In comparison with the statue of Gudea, the Susa vase is "minor art." Yet the richness of the incisions, encrusted with a white paste, the balance between the central scene of bird and fish and the design as a whole, and the pleasing rhythm of the various subsidiary geometric motifs reflect a highly developed artistic sensibility.

*Vase from Susa*
Circa 2000 B.C.
Terra cotta with incised decoration and encrusted with white paste; 7 1/2″ high. From Susa.

NAVAL EXPEDITION. *VIII Century B.C.*
The historical relief reappeared during the Late Assyrian period. The scene illustrated here represents the transportation of building materials destined for the royal palace at Khorsabad. The sculptor went into great detail. Several great beams are loaded on the decks of the ships, and others are being floated behind. The fleet passes in front of walled cities (the ports of Phoenicia). The whole scene is depicted from a bird's-eye view. The observer looks down onto the sea, its waves drawn in stylized spirals and striations. Interspersed among the ships appear fish, and genii in the form of human-headed bulls. Thus the viewer is asked to see beyond the ships and the surface of the water and look into another dimension, that of depth.

MAN–BULL AND INTERCEDING GODDESS. *End of the Second Millennium B.C.*
The Man-Bull and the goddess decorate a brick wall originally forming

*Man-Bull and Interceding Goddess*
Middle Elamite period; 1170–1151 B.C.
Brick relief; 54″ high.
From Susa.

*Naval Expedition*
Late Assyrian period. Reign of Sharruukin (Sargon) II: 721–705 B.C.
Alabaster; 115 1/4″ high.
From Dur Sharruukin (Khorsabad).

*Sacrificial Scene*
Larsa period: end of XX—beginning of XIX century B.C.
Fragment of mural from the Palace of Zimrilim at Mari (detail). Tempera on plaster; total height of fragment 31 1/2", 52" wide.

part of a building connected with a fertility cult. The goddess herself has hooves rather than hands. It is impossible to decide whether this slab formed part of a continuous frieze or if it alternated with pilasters.

DETAIL FROM A SACRIFICIAL SCENE. *Beginning of the Second Millennium B.C.*
During the Larsa Period (named after a city in Sumer), political power in Sumer was divided among a number of bickering city-states. Then Hammurabi of Babylon united the area under his rule after the fall of his greatest rival, the city of Mari, in 1897 B.C. The paintings in the palace of Mari, which was the home of the last king, Zimralim, appear to date from the period just before Hammurabi's conquest. Several sacrificial scenes were reconstructed from tiny fragments found in one of the two great courtyards of the palace. The detail illustrated here shows a procession of men leading a bull to the sacrifice. A giant figure of a god, king or priest leads a group of the devout. The design was executed in black outlines on a white background, with the addition of light and burnt ocher. On other murals in the same palace the artists used, in addition, red, yellow, blue and brown. While the artists are still conscious of principal views and registers of representation, they are not as constricted by them as were the Egyptians. Thus their art seems freer, less chained by convention and tradition. On the other hand, the strong profiles of the men depicted are clearly related to the canon of features developed already in Akkadian and Late-Sumerian sculpture and reliefs. This, the most ancient example of Mesopotamian wall painting we possess, obviously reflects a tradition already centuries old.

CODE OF HAMMURABI. *Beginning of the Second Millennium B.C.*
Hammurabi's famous Code of Laws is carved on most of the surface of this large basalt block. The discovery in Susa of the remains of a second example leads one to think that the code was carved on a number of such monuments and thus published among the principal cities of the kingdom. On the upper portion of the stele, King Hammurabi stands in front of a seated divinity and raises his right hand in a gesture of devotion. The god appears to be handing him a scepter, the sign of power. This motif of adoration is common on seals and has numerous antecedents in Late Sumerian monuments. Hammurabi's artists pay due homage to the culture he conquered, adopting the stylized schemes inherited from the monuments of the period of Gudea.

*Code of Hammurabi, King of Babylonia*
Late Larsa period: 1930–1888 B.C.
Detail. Black basalt; 88 1/2" high.
Stele from Susa: taken as war booty by Elamite King Sutruknahhunte in the XII century B.C.

*Propitiatory Genius of a Hero, Usually Identified as the Gilgamesh*
*Late Assyrian period; Reign of Sargon: 721–705 B.C. Alabaster; 166 1/2″* high. From the palace of Sargon II in Dur Sharruukin (Khorsabad): from the front of the throne room in one of the inner courts.

PROPITIATORY GENIUS OF A HERO. *End of the 8th Century B.C.* During the reign of Sargon II, Assyrian sculptors reached the height of their artistic expression in the powerful isolated figures of divinities, heroes, princes or genii. The genius illustrated here, linked by some with the hero Gilgamesh, exemplifies the massive strength of these figures. Although the figure is essentially geometric and frontal, it is animated by the coloristic carving of the hair (animal and human) and cloth, and the artist's feeling for expressive anatomical details.

ARCHERS OF THE PERSIAN GUARD. *V Century B.C.* The ancient Mesopotamian tradition of enameled brick, used by the Late Babylonians in Nebuchadnezzar's monumental Ishtar gate, was resumed by the Persian kings in the decoration of their luxurious palaces. Here, in stylized repetition, are shown the archers of Susa, the famous "Immortals," carrying lances with gold and silver tips.

*Archers of the Persian Guard*
Achemenide age: V century B.C.
Enameled bricks; height of each archer 57 4/5".
Frieze from the Palace of Darius in Susa.

LION. *IV Century B.C.*

Although Imperial Persian art owed a great deal to Assyria and Babylonia, it was open to numerous external influences; in this lion, and in the liveliness of its step, one senses a debt to Greek art. Yet the rhythmic interplay of curves which gives the muzzle its characteristic stylization departs from Assyrian tradition and reflects the influence of a linear sensibility originating in Central Asia. And, in turn, several centuries later, Chinese sculpture of the Liang period will feel the influence of the Achaemenian models on its own stylized lions.

*Lion*
Achemenide Age: IV century B.C.
Detail. Enameled bricks; length of the entire animal 145 2/5″. From Susa, formerly part of a "continuous" frieze.

# ANCIENT GREECE AND ROME

HEAD OF AN IDOL. *Circa 2000 B.C.*

In the Third and Second millennia B.C. the Cycladic Islands in the Aegean were inhabited by a civilization which preceded that of the Minoans in Crete. For the most part, the Cycladic culture belongs to the Bronze Age, but it does have close connections with the preceding Stone Age, from which it inherited the Mediterranean cult of the Mother-Goddess. In comparison with the opulent forms of the best-known of the Neolithic mother-goddesses, the Cycladic idols are distinguish by their severely geometric outlines, lack of plastic modeling and their schematization. At times a nascent naturalism appears to have been suppressed almost intentionally, as in the series of violin-shaped idols. The typical Cycladic figures are more related to relief sculpture than to statues. Their heads are in the shape of large shields, the long necks are rounded, the bodies are upside-down triangles, with the base at the shoulders and the tip at the ankles; their arms are simple crossed lines and breasts, just little dots. The separation of the legs is indicated by a line which does not pierce through the stone. The idols are usually quite small and cut out of white marble. Sometimes facial features were added in paint. The extreme stylization is perhaps more a matter of esthetic choice than the result of limits imposed by the artists' skills, for these figures have been found in tombs with idols of a much more substantial corporeality.

The head illustrated here, from Amorgos, belonged to a figurine of exceptional size and workmanship. Now that it is separated from its body, its abstractness becomes even more striking—pure form or pure symbol according to the taste and viewpoint of the observer. Perhaps a formalist approach is the more legitimate, for the real meaning lies buried with the civilization which created it, while the form is as apparent to us today as it was to the artist who made it so many millennia ago. Thus one can understand the influence this head had on the first post-Cubist generation of abstract sculptors, including Archipenko, Arp and Brancusi.

*Head of an Idol*
Circa 2000 B.C.
Marble; height of fragment: 10 1/2″.
From the island of Amorgos, Cyclades.

WORKSHOP OF PHIDIAS—PANATHENAIC PROCESSION.
*V Century B.C.*

The continuous frieze which ran around the cella of the Parthenon (within the peristyle) was executed by a team of sculptors and craftsmen under the direction of Phidias. The marbles of the Parthenon represent the high point of Greek art, when a perfect balance had been achieved between realism and the architectonic elements. The artists were still working within the stylistic conventions developed in the Archaic period, but they were elaborating on their heritage. The Panathenaic frieze characterizes the Greek concept of relief, which is born of a graphic tradition and seeks to give itself sculptural rather than two-dimensional, linear forms. The relief field is only two figures deep. When the artists wished to enlarge this shallow field, they used the old convention of indicating a horizontal expansion rather than penetrating the background visually. This is evident in the thrones of the gods at

PHIDIAS (workshop)
*Panathenaic Procession*
447–432 B.C.
Pentelic marble; 41 1/3″ high.
Section from frieze of the eastern part of Parthenon with maidens giving two officials of the procession the official robes as an offering to Athena.

the east end of the frieze. Thus the background retains the same spatial value of every point in the frieze.

Every figure and every group has the same value in the balance between occupied and unoccupied spaces throughout the frieze. This harmony is exemplified by the magnificent series of *peplophoroi* (wearers of the ceremonial Panathenaean festival robes) and the strong verticals of their drapery, which mark the rhythm of the whole procession honoring Athens' Athena.

VENUS OF MILOS. *II Century B.C.*
The Venus found on the island of Milos attests the vitality of Hellenistic art during the century which also saw the production of the Pergamum Altar masterpieces. Her stylized elegance can be called

*Venus of Milos*
Second half of II century B.C.
Detail. Parian marble; 80 1/3″ high.
From island of Milos, discovered in 1820 and in the Louvre since 1821.

manneristic in the intentional contrast of the softness of female flesh with the deep shadows and rich texture of her heavy drapery—a contrast also reminiscent of the Pergamum sculpture. The artist treated feminine beauty with great warmth and understanding, and worked easily within the concept of rounded three-dimensional rather than four-faced figures. The classical artists had striven to reach this point, and the Hellenistic master reaped the fruits of their struggle.

VICTORY OF SAMOTHRACE. *Circa 190 B.C.*
The Winged Victory of Samothrace was connected for a number of years with the naval victory of Demetrius Poliorcetes in 306, and then more persuasively to the Rhodian conquest of Antiochus III (222–187 B.C.). The style justifies the later dating. The Victory is a spectacular piece. Her body is thrust forward by the giant wings and the sea wind catches her drapery which, dampened by the salt spray, clings to her body. The light chiton adheres to her breasts, and her cloak, slipping from her shoulders, wraps around her legs and billows out behind her. The treatment of the cloth is related to the so-called 'wet drapery' of the post-Phidian period, but in its exaggerated curves and chiaroscuro effect it is almost baroque, which again justifies the later dating.

*Victory of Samothrace*
Circa 190 B.C.
Parian marble; 108 1/3″ high.
Discovered in Samothrace in 1863.

FEMALE PORTRAIT. *II Century A.D.*
The portraits from Fayum (which also have been found elsewhere in Egypt) are the only "easel paintings" preserved to us from classical antiquity. They date from the first to the fourth centuries A.D., and approximately 500 are extant, scattered in museums all over the world. Most of them belong to a current of expressionistic popular art which is Coptic rather than Greco-Roman. Although the portraits were used on sarcophagi, as in the old Egyptian tradition, they were probably painted during the owner's lifetime. For the most part, the paintings were executed on board in the encaustic technique, where melted colored bees wax was spread on the surface of the wood with a spatula (although there are a few instances in tempera, and on cloth). Colors in wax are difficult to manipulate and to dilute, so that the portraits compare unfavorably with works done in the more versatile water paint mediums. The artists had to work in dabs and short strokes, creating forms without an outline in a technique which particularly lends itself to luministic effects.

This delicate portrait of a girl dates no earlier than the reign of Hadrian (if it really comes from Antinoë), and is related to the Hellenistic tradition of portraying the middle class along with philosophers, poets and statesmen. The highlights in the eyes, along the nose and on the upper lip as well as the shimmer of gold in the hair remind one of the delicate lighting and the golds in a Titian, a Velazquez or a Goya.

*On page 60*

*Female Portrait*
II century A.D.
Detail. Encaustic; 16 1/2″ high, 9 2/5″ wide. From Fayum, Egypt, more accurately, probably from the excavations at Antinoöpolis: acquired by the Louvre in 1953.

## PERSIA
## CHRISTIAN EGYPT
## BYZANTIUM

BYZANTINE ART IN ROME. *The Story of Jonah.*
According to the Bible, Jonah was cast into the sea to placate the tempest which God had raised against him, whereupon he was swallowed by a marine monster in whose stomach he stayed for three days before being vomited up on a beach. According to the interpretation of early Christians, this story prefigured the death and resurrection of Christ in particular and of all the Christians in general. The Byzantine representation in this gold-leaf design on a fragment of a ritual cup is enclosed by a stylized frame symbolizing a great wave (following a similar convention for decorating the insides of pots). Within, a Roman ship with a large square rig appears in the upper zone; and below is shown the whale swallowing the prophet, the curve of his body echoing that of the keel and emphasizing the curve of the cup. Iconographically the representation is very close to that of the Lateran *Jonah Sarcophagus,* which dates from the end of the third-century A.D.

SASSANIAN ART. *Horse's Head.*
The silver horse's head is characteristic of third to fourth-century art—the interest in animal motifs, the liveliness and vitality of their execution, a quasi-calligraphic pleasure in geometric design and the taste for trappings covered with ornament of Oriental derivation. A certain Greek, or Western influence is also apparent in the corporeality of the horse's head.

SASSANIAN ART
*Head of a Horse* (4th–5th century)
Relief and incised silver, gilt with mercury; 5 1/2″ × 7 3/4″. Fragment from Kirman.

BYZANTINE ART IN ROME
*Jonah* (3rd–4th century)
Diameter; 4 1/4″. Incised gold sheet between two sheets of glass. Its circular, concave shape shows it to have belonged originally to a cup, used for ritual purposes. From a cemetery in Rome. The Greek inscription, "Zesis," is frequently found on glassware of this type.

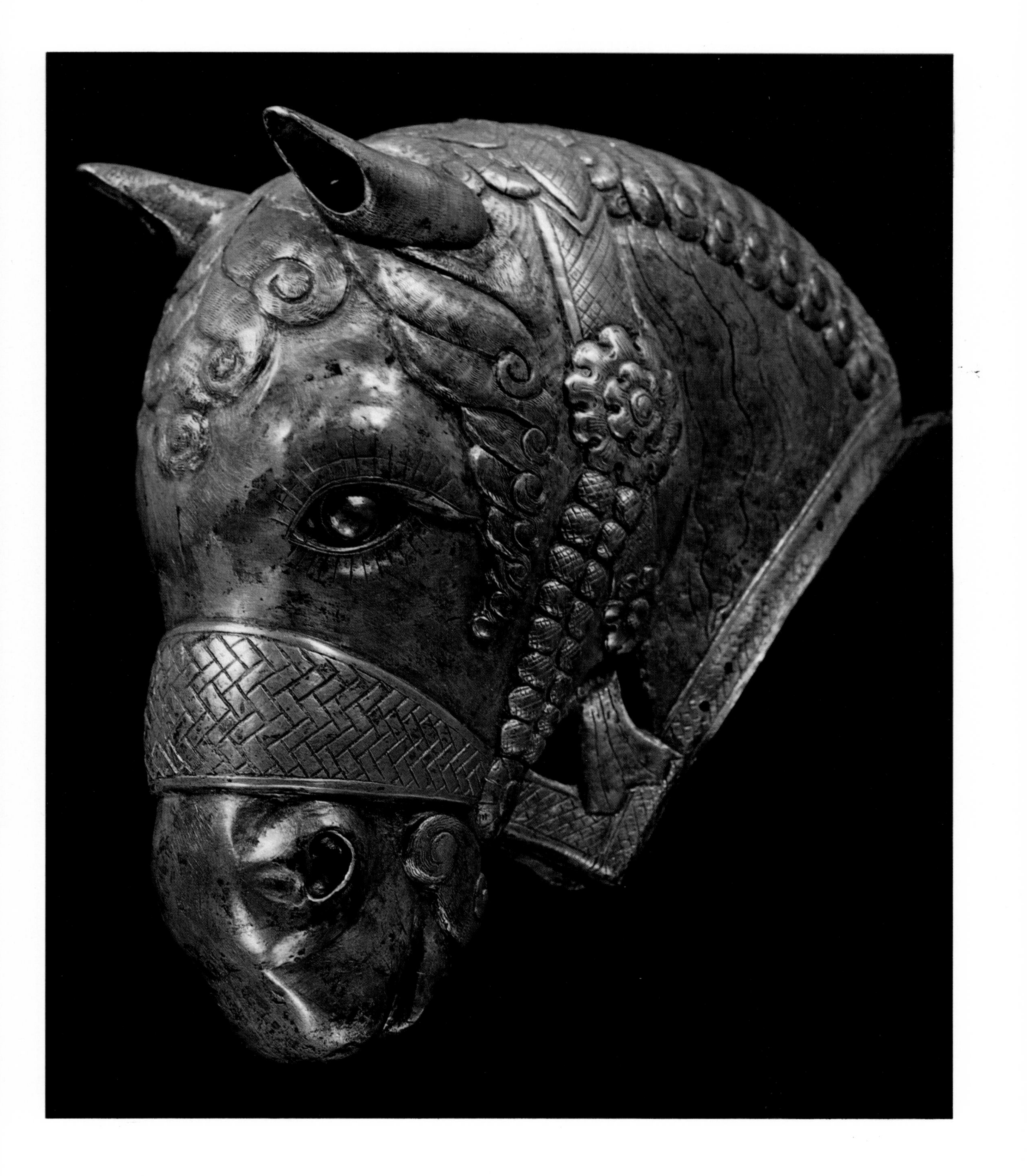

BYZANTINE ART. *Hunting Scene.*

While the subject and the technique of this Byzantine plaque are common, it has a special freshness, particularly in the attention paid to the detail of its lively tri-colored composition. Three hunters, two mounted and one on foot, all armed with lances, pursue several wild beasts.

One of them, a lion in the center of the composition, turns on a horseman. The hunter pivots about with the impetuous courage of those heroes depicted in the reliefs on Hellenistic sarcophagi. The movement of the composition follows an ideal structure in the shape of a sigma, and the representation is characterized by the artist's keen sense for the play of light, as seen in his use of gold and silver. The plaque illustrates the exquisite late Alexandrian taste of artist and patron.

BYZANTINE ART
*Hunting Scene* (5th–6th century)
Small rectangular plaque, gilt bronze with silver inlays drilled and punched, 7 1/4″ × 6″. The holes at the corners and the traces of a frame show it was originally an ornamental appliqué, probably for some piece of furniture.

COPTIC ART. *Daphne (?).*
The identification of this figure as Daphne is suggested by the leaves which frame her bust. The monument is part of a group of Coptic sculptures found in centers far from Alexandria and characterized by traces of Indian, Syrian, Armenian and Persian influences—that is, those cultures which are considered in general as contributing to the formation of Coptic art. Although this relief has obvious ties with Western art, the artist's attitude was basically anti-classical, as is evident in his use of Near-Eastern canons of proportion. The figure is inscribed in a pentagon, whose axes control the placement and detail of the woman's body. At the center of the pentagon glitters the large pendant of her necklace. The relief probably was placed somewhat above the observer's head since it looks best when viewed from below. The ideal center of the composition is the face, remarkable for its serenity and sweetness.

COPTIC ART. *Sea Goddess and Water Games.*
At the center of the textile appears a sea goddess (Venus?) framed by a wave motif done in perspective, suggesting the movement of the sea. Her head is set against a nimbus and crowned with a diadem. Outside the central medallion four nereids are depicted playing in the sea, accompanied by sea lions and fish. The whole is more decorative than narrative. Both the composition and the colors relate to the monumental elegance of mosaic floors. The classical themes, transmitted by Alex-

COPTIC ART
*Daphne* (5th–6th century)
Marble relief, 10 1/4″ × 8 1/4″.
Fragment from *Sheh Abahd.* The figure originally seems to have worn a ribbon on its head. The hands held the ends of a ribbon; the arms were outstretched.

andria and frequent in Coptic art, are reinterpreted with lively imagination. They lasted well beyond the coming of Christianity to Egypt.

COPTIC ART. *Dionysos, with Motifs from the Cult of Isis.*
A giant Dionysos appears on the left side of the composition, carrying his thyrsus and surrounded by vines. He stands rather casually watching a ritual of the mysteries of Isis, as the symbol of the moon would indicate. Both the episodic character of the design, not easily explained as it stands alone, and the asymmetry of the representation suggest that this is only a portion of a more complex composition.

COPTIC ART. *Portrait of a Young Girl.*
A young girl is represented lying on her coffin. In her left hand she holds the symbol of Isis, which has become a Christian emblem, and it reappears by her feet. Her right hand is raised in a gesture of leave-taking. The realism of the head recalls that of the famous Fayum series. Here, however, the facial expression is distinguished by its greater composure and even resignation. The rest of the body is as stylized as a mummy. This shroud had to cover the sides of the corpse as well as the top, and the artist modified the decoration accordingly. We see the body from above, in a bird's eye view, while the sides are depicted flattened out, showing peacocks—symbol of immortality—and a row of leaves decorating the borders.

*Above:*
COPTIC ART
*Dionysos, with Motifs from the Cult of Isis*
(6th century)
Woven cloth, wool on linen, probably from Antinoë, 22 3/4″ × 21 3/4″.

*Left:*
COPTIC ART
*Sea Goddess and Water Games*
V century. Textile panel; 11 3/4″ wide.
From the von Clédat Collection.

COPTIC ART
*Portrait of Young Girl Lying Down*
(second half of 3rd century)
Fragment of a sheet painted in encaustic. From the excavations at Gayel. 85″ × 35 3/4″.

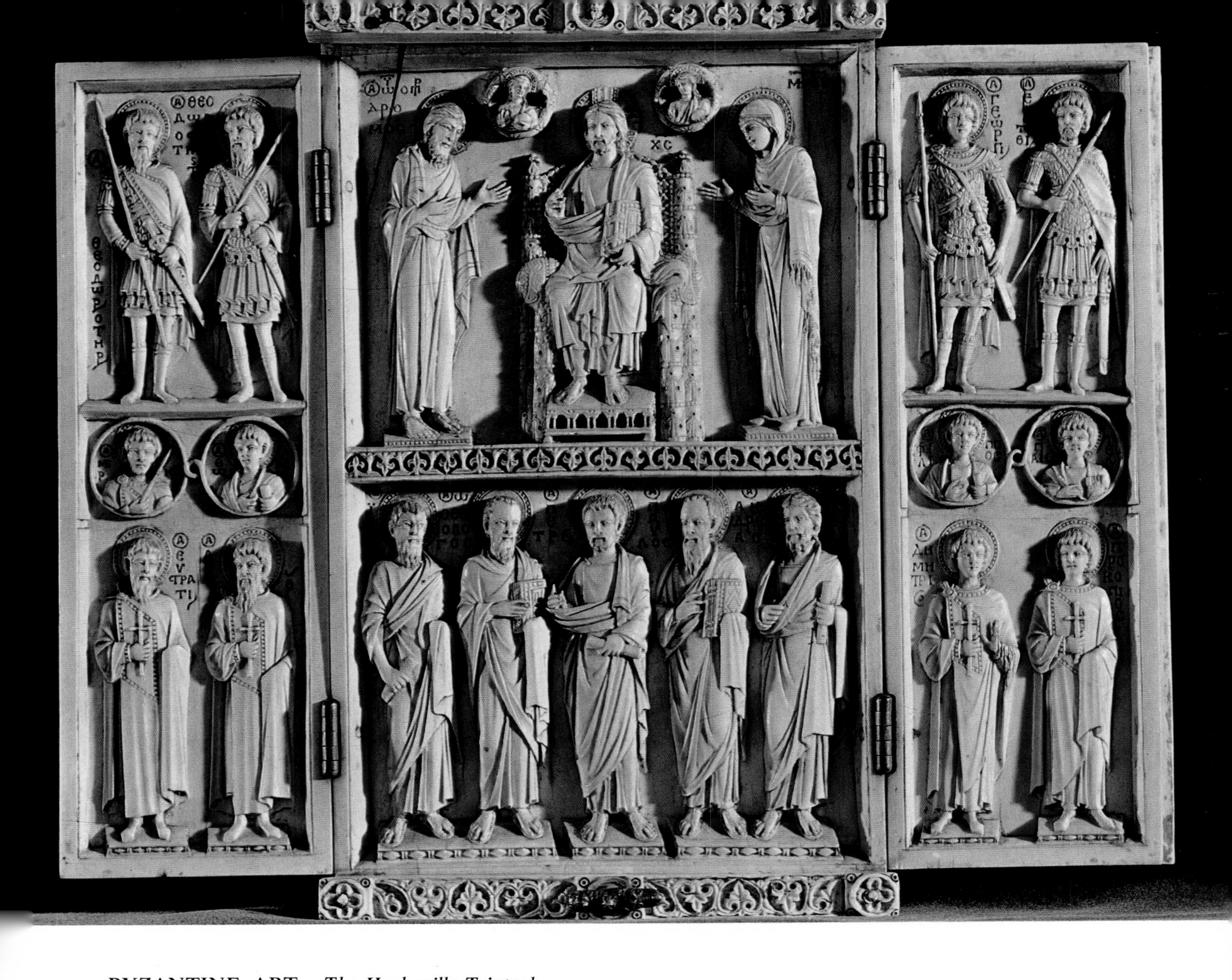

BYZANTINE ART. *The Harbaville Triptych.*

The Harbaville Triptych is a miniature portable icon. The central panel is divided into two superimposed registers by an ornament which is repeated with the addition of rosettes at the lower edge and of three little heads at the top. In the center of the upper register, Christ is shown seated on an ivory throne flanked by the Virgin and St. John standing in attitudes of worship. Above, on either side of Christ's head are a pair of medallions out of which peer angels holding the symbols of the sun and the moon, typical of imperial iconography. In the lower register stand five Apostles, dressed in classical togas. The shutters at left and right are perfectly symmetrical, with four warriors in the two upper registers, and eight saints below, four in medallions and four full-length wearing the dress of civilian dignitaries. The triptych exemplifies the revival of the ancient art of ivory carving; it has been assigned to the fifth century A.D., although a more acceptable date would be the tenth century, judging from the style of the Deisis.

BYZANTINE ART
*Harbaville Triptych* (10th century)
Small portable altar, ivory. Central panel, 9 1/2″ × 5 1/2″; side panels, 8 1/2″ × 2 3/4″. The name refers to the collection to which it belonged, in Arras, before coming to the Louvre.

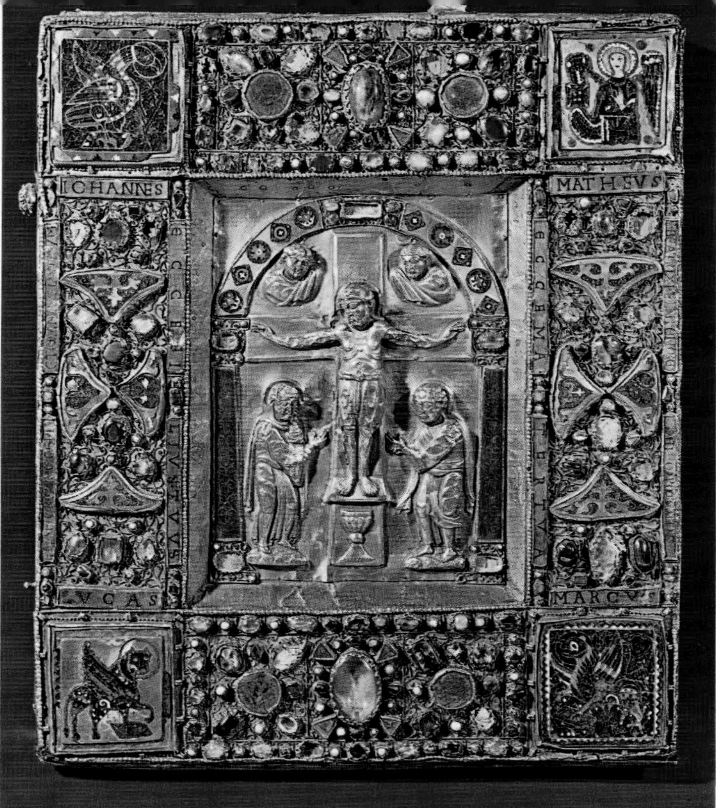


SYRIAN ART
*Christ Blessing* (5th–6th century)
Silver relief, partly gilt tondo. Diameter 6″.
Crowning element of a cross. (?)

OTTONIAN ART
*Binding for a Gospel Book*
(circa 9th century)
Gold relief, decorated with inset glass, stones, enamel, filigree and cameos. 15 3/4″ × 13″. From the Abbey of St. Denis. It was perhaps a gift from Beatrice, daughter of Hugues Capet. The inscription, restored and damaged, along the outer border reads as follows: "Beatrix me in onore Dei omnipotentis et omnium sanctorum eius fieri precepi."

SYRIAN ART. *Christ Blessing.*
This silver tondo depicts the beardless Christ Pantocrator, following the Syrian tradition, according to which the book should be inscribed with the phrase *"Ego sum lux mundi, qui sequitur me non ambulat in tenebris."* The frame of pearls is probably a stylized representation of clouds, out of which Christ emerges clad in a toga. This type becomes canonical for centuries, an expression of geometric severity and majesty. The only element in motion is Christ's hand, curved into a stylized gesture of benediction.

OTTONIAN ART (?). *Binding for a Gospel Book.*
The origins of sumptuous objects of this type, with their mixed techniques, are difficult to determine: this Gospel Book binding has been alternately assigned to a Byzantine workshop of the Macedonian school and to Ottonian studios. In the central panel the theme of the Crucifixion is depicted with the Virgin and St. John at either side of the cross, above which appear the symbols of the sun and the moon. This central theme is framed by recessed planes in perspective, surrounded by a wide band of ornamentation, including the symbols of the Evangelists with their names in each corner. The binding is related to the Reliquary of St. Foy at Conques or the Portable Altar of S. Andrea at Treviri, both of which embody the major characteristics of the brilliant Ottonian school of goldsmiths.

BYZANTINE ART. *Transfiguration.*
The rigid iconography of the Transfiguration, from the Dalmatian Carolingian epoch to Raphael, demanded that the representation be organized according to the axial coordinates of the miraculous appari-

BYZANTINE ART
*Transfiguration* (12th century)
Mosaic of stones and glass paste on wax base; 20 1/2″ × 14″. Can be dated 12th century, but with later restorations.

tion. In this miniature mosaic, stylization of the accessory details—landscape, drapery, gestures, the frozen symbolism of the mandorlas and rays—when fused with the realism of the facial expressions heighten the sense of pathos and place the work among the ideal prototypes for Trecento painting and Cimabue. The icon, intended for domestic use, probably came from Constantinople.

RUSSIAN ART. *Last Judgment.*
The detail illustrated here is part of a large panel representing the Last Judgment, Paradise, Hell and the Militant and the Triumphant Church, all according to medieval Byzantine iconography. This detail shows an angel thrusting aside the firmament which bears the symbol of the sun, accompanied by the angelic host. Flanked by the symbol of the Holy Spirit, God the Father is shown seated in the tondo, calling His Son to sit at His side. Below, Christ sits on His throne in judgment, surrounded by the Tetramorphs (symbols of the Four Evangelists) and flanked by Mary and the Precursor John the Baptist, who present to him the kneeling Adam and Eve. The painting, in keeping with the rigid orthodox liturgy, typifies conservative religious art in its iconography as well as in its five centuries of Byzantine style.

RUSSIAN ART
*Last Judgment* (17th century)
Detail. Tempera and oil on panel. Entire panel measures 77″ × 57″. Probably from Moscow.

# FRANCE

BURGUNDIAN ART. *Descent from the Cross.*
The figure of Christ illustrated here originally formed part of a sculptural ensemble representing the Deposition. Although we know of no other examples in France itself, a number occur in Italy and these divide into two distinct types, one characterized by its realism (as at Norcia, Pescia, Tivoli and Volterra) and the other by its use of symbolism and by the appearance of the Virgin and St. John only (as at S. Miniato al Tedesco). In general the Italian examples are somewhat later than the French. Christ's elongated, almost serpentine body was the focal point in a composition remarkable for its refined, attenuated elegance. The effect is enhanced by the decorative quality of the hair framing the face and ending in curls on the shoulders, the wavy strands of the beard, and the carefully indicated folds of the drapery. Originating from the region of Burgundy, this figure is more closely related to the Last Judgment on the portal at Autun than to the Christ of the narthex at Vezelay. The drapery of the latter gives the figure a restless movement, similar to some of the more poignant *Pietà* representations. Whereas in the Autun Christ as well as the sculpture illustrated here the folds simply outline and accentuate the body, giving through their rhythms a note of serenity to the pathos of this image of divine lamentation.

HENRI BELLECHOSE (?). *Last Communion and Martyrdom of St. Denis.*
This painting is a typical example of "mixed" narrative, or, following Wickhoff's definition, a "continuous narrative." It consists of the repetition of the same figure in the same surroundings taking part in diverse situations. Although thus broken down, the narrative maintains an emphasis on a central sacred theme, which in size and importance overshadows all the others, thus becoming, in a sense, "discontinuous." Finally, both the continuous and discontinuous are united in symbolical function through the addition of certain attributes—such as that of the angelic host—which stem from the identification in medieval France of the St. Denis, who was first bishop of Paris and protector of France, with Denis the Areopagite, a disciple of St. Paul and a theological interpreter of the nature of angels.

To the left, St. Denis receives communion from the hand of Christ. On the right side, he is beheaded along with Saints Rusticus and Eleutherius, and in the center is shown the Trinity. The composition borrows its structure from the iconography of the Crucifixion. It is bathed in golden sunbeams streaming down from heaven, giving it the aura of a miraculous vision. A marked interest in the psychology of the facial expression, together with a certain sweetness point to a possible influence from the North Italian Trecento.

BURGUNDIAN ART
*Descent from the Cross*
(12th century)
Painted and gilt wood. The left arm is a modern restoration. 61″ × 66 1/4″.

HENRI BELLECHOSF
Brabant (?)—Dijon 1440–1444
*Last Communion and Martyrdom of St. Denis*
(between 1398 and 1416)
Tempera on panel, 63 1/2″ × 82 3/4″.
From the Charterhouse of Champmol.

SCHOOL OF AVIGNON. *Pietà.*

Despite its fame, this Pietà remains of uncertain attribution and date; it it is assigned by some to a Spanish or Portuguese painter, by others to an Italianate artist working in the tradition of Rogier van der Weyden. Ragghianti and Sterling assign it to Enguerrand de Charrenton. The painting has been dated by some to the 1470's; others consider 1457 a date *ante quem,* since the Pietà of Tarragon, which included the same detail of St. John removing the thorns from Jesus' head, was completed that year. The praying figure at the left belongs to the Flemish tradition of incisive portraiture. The figures of the mourners stand out as if carved in ivory against an immense sky of gold, and the outlines of a dream city, with a distinctly Islamic appearance, arise on the far horizon. In their architectonic lines, these figures descend from a long tradition of Pietàs in sculpture. They bend over Christ to form a sort of living canopy, while the praying donor is set off from the group by the unyielding verticality of his genuflection. Christ's body, a long fluid silhouette whose pallor stands in striking contrast to the dark background of cloth, lies on His mother's knees as in a *Vesperbild,* the lines of its pathetic abandon accentuated by the long inscription.

SCHOOL OF AVIGNON
*Pietà* (15th century) Oil and tempera on panel, 63 3/4″ × 85 3/4″. From the Charterhouse of Villeneuve-les-Avignons.

JEAN FOUQUET. *Charles VII, King of France.*
The king is depicted in kneeling attitude looking out of a chapel window whose curtains are pulled aside, as if he were participating in a religious ceremony. Although at first sight the painting appears to be a votive portrait, the inscription written on the frame (which imitates the window jambs) refers to the king as *"très victorieux."* Thus it appears to be a commemorative portrait, probably commissioned after the Truce of Arras in 1444 or after the battle of Formigny, both being events which would justify calling him "victorious." In all probability, the portrait was executed after Fouquet's voyage to Italy between 1444 and 1447.

The painting marks the debut of this portrait type in France. It harks back to prototypes in the circle of van Eyck, with some concessions to the Bohemian tradition, especially in the three-quarter position of the body on a light background and in the king's rich attire (compare for example the portrait of the Emperor Sigismund in the Vienna Museum, attributed to Pisanello), and to late Treccento Italy. During his trip to Italy, Fouquet must have visited Verona, where the memory of a great courtly tradition still survived, as in the works of Altichiero, who had a particular influence on Fouquet's miniatures, and of Pisanello.

ANONYMOUS FRENCH MASTER. *The Beautiful Gabrielle and the Maréchale de Balagny.*
During the 16th century in France, portrait painting enjoyed a special favor in court circles. Portraits were sent as gifts on numerous occasions, above all for weddings. In this painting, Gabrielle d'Estrée and her sister are shown taking a bath together, a fashionable theme at the time. The picture probably contains an allusion to the fertility of Gabrielle and her projected marriage with Henry IV. The ivory-like figures are framed by the curtains held back over their heads. A domestic scene in the background shows a woman sewing, seated in the warmth of a fireplace.

The influence of Clouet is strong in this work, which belongs to the later years of the School of Fontainebleau, perhaps around 1596, when Gabrielle, the king's mistress, was expecting a baby. At the latest, the picture could date from 1599, when she died in childbirth. The portrait is more interesting perhaps from the point of view of cultural history than of art, and projects a sense of intimacy, allowing an insight into the lives of these elegant French ladies.

JEAN FOUQUET
Tours 1420—died between 1477 and 1481
*Charles VII, King of France*
Panel, 33 3/4" × 28 1/4".
From the Ste. Chapelle of Bourges.

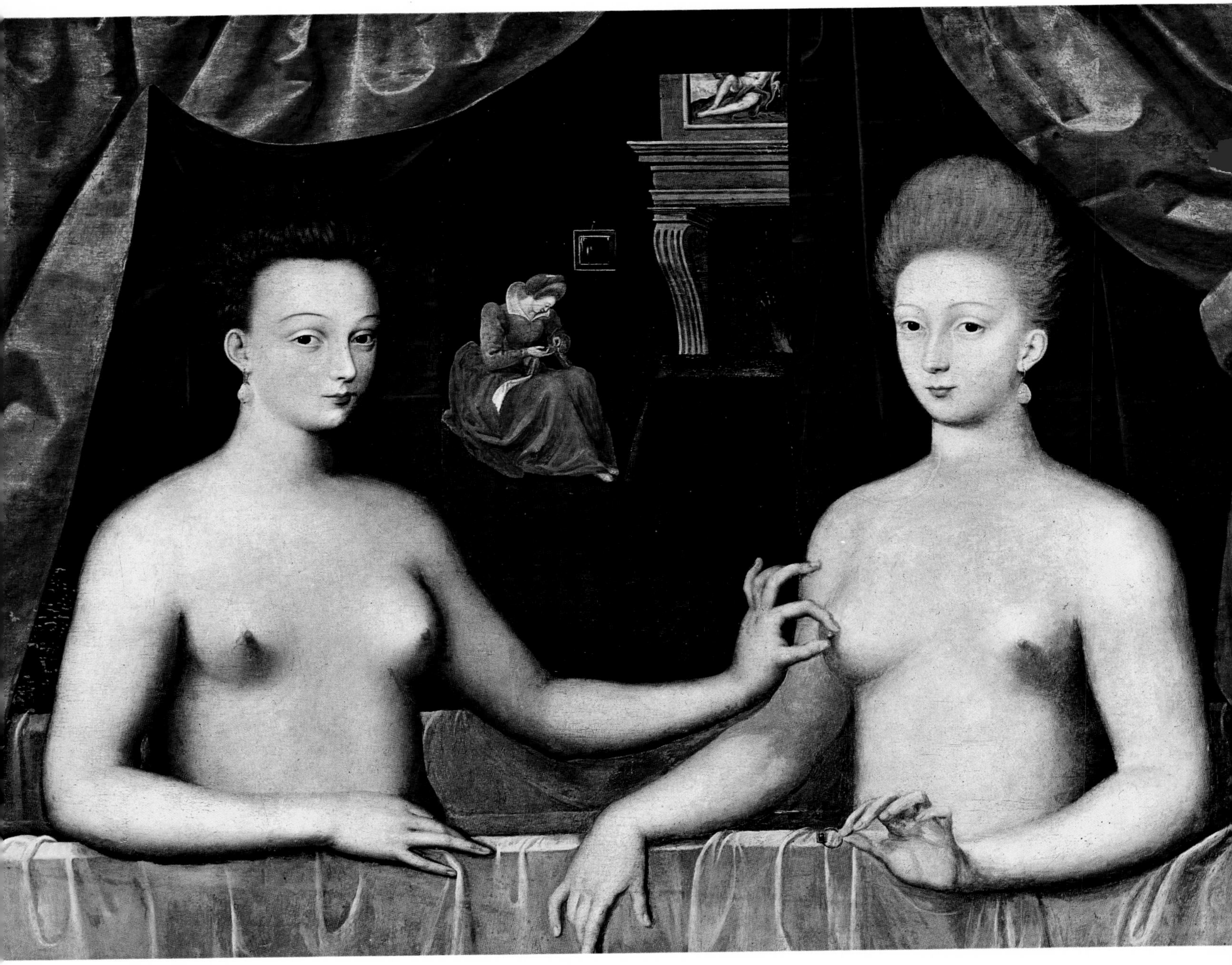

GERMAIN PILON. *Statue of the Cardinal de Birague.*
By the time he was commissioned to do this statue, Pilon had already enjoyed a certain vogue at court during his youth. Along with other works, he executed the statues for the tomb of Henry II and Catherine de' Medici at the cathedral of St. Denis, under the direction of Primaticcio. The memorial statue of Cardinal de Birague represents a turning point in Pilon's art. He abandoned the Mannerism of his earlier works and attempted a more realist approach. The deceased cardinal is shown on his knees, enveloped in the heavy folds of his garments. His attitude of intense devotion is emphasized by the inflexibility of his posture. The artist devoted most of his attention to a profound analysis of the man's physiognomy, as detailed and as precise as a life mask.

ANONYMOUS FRENCH
*The Beautiful Gabrielle and the Maréchale de Balagny* (circa 1596)
Panel, 37 3/4" × 49 1/4".

GERMAIN PILON
Paris 1537—1590
*Statue of Cardinal de Birague* (1584–85)
Detail. Bronze, 56 1/4" × 76 3/4".
Cardinal René de Birague, who was Chancellor of France, died in 1583; his tomb was commissioned by his daughter, the Marquise de Nesle.

BAUGIN
Documented circa 1630
*Still-life with Pastries*
(circa 1630) 20 1/2″ × 15 3/4″.

GEORGES DE LA TOUR. *Mary Magdalene with Oil Lamp.*

Georges de La Tour painted two pictures of the saint, the one illustrated here and *Mary Magdalene at Her Mirror* in the Fabius Collection. Both pictures show a woman absorbed in meditation, with hand resting on a skull by the light of a lamp which just barely illuminates a darkly shadowed space. The use of the same model and the very slight variation in subject matter suggest a close relation between the pictures.

The art of La Tour is nostalgically reminiscent of the Quattrocento in the sculptural compactness of its forms and in its restrained luminosity. More decisive, however, was the influence of Caravaggio, which according to some, La Tour felt during a trip to Rome around 1612–13. According to others, it came to him through the Flemish and Lorraine Caravaggesques (like Le Clerc), also from Honthorst, whom La Tour might have met on a trip to Holland. His acquaintance with the latter's work is reflected principally in the manipulation of light, which springs from a source within the picture itself and thus participates more naturalistically in the representation of a whole. Finally, the works of Terbrugghen were an important influence on La Tour.

In the painting of Mary Magdalene, as in all La Tour's canvases, there is a sense of cheerless solitude and despondent immobility which is in keeping with the morose and withdrawn nature of the artist.

GEORGES DE LA TOUR
Vic 1593—Lunéville 1652
*Mary Magdalen with Oil Lamp*
(1635–1640)
Detail. Oil on canvas; 50 1/2″ × 37″.

BAUGIN. *Still-life with Pastries.*

Baugin signed a group of still-lifes among which is included the Louvre example. During the reigns of Henry IV and Louis XIII, a colony of

NICOLAS POUSSIN. *The Inspiration of the Poet.*
Although the subject of this painting is difficult to interpret, it concerns an allegorical celebration of epic poetry, as suggested by the presence of the muse Calliope, recognizable through her resemblance to her description in Father Ripa's treaty on iconography, and by the titles of the books in the foreground—the *Odyssey,* the *Iliad* and the *Aeneid.* The painting can hardly have been executed in honor of a contemporary poet as the inspired mortal bears no resemblance to any writers dear to the artist or to any of his friends, such as Ariosto, Tasso or Marino. The subject might be Apollo crowning Virgil, since the poet in the painting resembles a figure which appears on the frontispiece of the Virgil published by the *Imprimerie Royale* in 1641, an engraving by Claude Mellan after Poussin. The date of the picture too has caused some problems, although that proposed by Blunt—before 1630—seems likely. Poussin painted another picture with the same theme, with Euterpe, the muse of lyric poetry, and a poet identifiable as Anacreon. These depictions of the varieties of classical poetry go back iconographically and stylistically—in the evocation of mythology as well as in pictorial tradition—to Paolo Veronese, Titian and above all to Raphael, whose *Parnassus* in the Vatican furnished a striking precedent. Poussin's work is reminiscent of Raphael's, possessing the same quality of revery and exaltation. Apollo, crowned with a laurel wreath, sits in the center, his arm resting on his cithara. He is making a slow, solemn gesture as he dictates to the inspired poet, reflecting the theories of Plato's *Phaedrus.* At the god's side stands the muse, a flute in hand. Above and below, a pair of putti distribute wreaths. This painting, justly considered one of Poussin's finest, is dominated by the poetic exaltation of the figures, heightened by an ample, almost epic landscape of heaven and earth framing god, man and muse.

NICOLAS POUSSIN
Les Andelys 1594—Rome 1665
*The Inspiration of the Poet* (before 1630)
Oil on canvas; 72 1/2" × 84 1/4". The painting can be identified with the one formerly in Mazarin's collection, admired by Bernini in 1665, as mentioned by Chantelou.

NICOLAS POUSSIN. *Self-Portrait.* *p. 88*
Poussin painted two self-portraits, probably planned together and executed at about the same time. One, painted in 1649 for Pointel, is now in the Museum of East Berlin, while a copy (?) is in the Gimpel Collection, London. The Louvre picture, begun in September of the same year and finished in 1650, was painted for the artist's friend and patron Paul Fréart de Chantelou. While the Berlin example is romantic, even Baroque, the Louvre painting, with a corner of the artist's studio and a pile of his works appearing in the background, is more severely classic.

NICOLAS POUSSIN
Les Andelys 1594—Rome 1665
*Self-Portrait* (1650)
Oil on canvas; 38 1/2″ × 18 1/2″. Bears the following inscription: "Effigies Nicolai Poussini Andelyensis pictoris. Anno aetatis 56. Romae anno jubilei 1650."

Although the artist's position before his mirror is the same in both pictures, in the first Poussin shows himself more animated and elegantly dressed. He rests his hand on a book titled *De lumine et colore*. In the background there appears a frieze decorated in relief with putti and laurel festoons. The Louvre portrait is more purely documentary, showing the artist's studio with his pictures leaning against each other in a beautifully geometric pattern. The artist's clothing is simpler, instead of a book he holds a portfolio of sketches and his face has a solemn, impassive expression. Poussin probably intended to offer two examples of "modes" or manners of painting, chosen by the artist according to the requirements of the occasion. Here he uses the so-called "Phrygian" and "Doric" mode. The choice of mode for a portrait probably depended on the sitter's interests and taste. As a matter of fact, Poussin consigned this picture to Chantelou probably because it seemed to him a truer likeness.

CLAUDE LORRAIN. *Ulysses Returning Chryseis to Her Father.*
The mythological subject of this picture is simply a pretext for a landscape of immense proportions, its vastness emphasized by the small scale of the figures. The scene of the reconciliation takes place at the left, on the stairs leading to a classical palace, reminiscent of Pietro da Cortona. Beyond a large Mediterranean pine appears a Roman villa,

CLAUDE GELÉE
(CLAUDE LORRAIN)
Chamagne 1600—Rome 1682
*Ulysses Returns Chryseis to Her Father*
(circa 1644)
Detail. Oil on canvas.
47″ × 59″.

then a medieval port tower. The whole gives the impression of a mythic townscape permeated with seventeenth-century buoyancy. In the harbor, a galleon rides at anchor, casting a long shadow on the water. To the right is a building remarkable for its gigantic orders, crowded together in a manner reminiscent of Bernini. A strip of light divides the background from the foreground, where the artist shows the activity characteristic of a port—boats, merchants, goods and sailors.

Although a contemporary of Poussin, Lorrain reverses the latter's vision and sentiment. He raised landscape to the level of a protagonist, reduced the importance of the human figure and abandoned himself to a dream of utopian surroundings, the thought of a golden age, without Poussin's Cartesian discipline, without his melancholy or restlessness.

ETIENNE-MAURICE FALCONET. *Bather.*
The *Bather* is a typical example of Rococo decorative statuary, destined to adorn the boudoirs of ladies and cardinals. The girl stepping into a pool is more a nymph than a real figure, inspired by the mythological imagination of the period, as in the poetics of Boucher. Already, however, one can sense a breath of cool Neo-Classicism.

In the year he finished this famous statue, Falconet found his true vocation. He became the director of the celebrated porcelain factory at Sèvres. His patroness was Mme. de Pompadour, whom he once portrayed as Venus Anadyomene. His works of this type, although drawing-room frivolities, are distinguished by their harmonious elegance and poetic delicacy.

ETIENNE-MAURICE FALCONET
Paris 1716–1791
*Bather* (1756–57)
Marble. 32″ high. Once thought to have been sculpted for Tiroux d'Epersenne (allegedly exhibited in the *Salon* in 1757), it is now believed to have belonged to the Countess du Barry and to have come to the Louvre after the confiscation of her property during the Revolution.

FRANÇOIS BOUCHER. *Diana Resting.*
A pupil of Watteau, Boucher was a highly gifted, hard-working painter, a virtuoso of the brush. Five years after Diana was exhibited at the Salon, he was granted the patronage of Mme. de Pompadour, and to a certain extent became the paradigm of the Louis XV style. Diderot was his only opponent, expressing a preference for Chardin.

*Diana Resting* appears to reflect Boucher's Italian visit, especially in the goddess's golden nudity, of an impalpable softness inspired by Correggio and of a delicate fantasy inspired by Ricci's Arcadian visions.

ANTOINE WATTEAU. *The Embarkation for Cythera.*
With this picture Watteau was admitted to the Royal Academy of Painting and Sculpture in 1717. For this honor, he had waited since his original application in 1712. It took him five years to present this work to the Academy, and even then it had not assumed its final form. A little after 1717, resuming this same theme, he created a more finished work which was purchased by Julienne (it is in Berlin). The picture has enjoyed wide fame, as echoed in the words of the Goncourts, who in their book on eighteenth-century art called it the masterpiece of French masterpieces.

In this picture, Watteau reveals that he has matured through a study of

FRANÇOIS BOUCHER
Paris 1703–1770
*Diana Resting* (1742)
Detail. 22 1/2″ × 28 3/4″.

Rubens, whose influence is evident in the thick brushstrokes, and of the drawings of Bassano, Titian and van Dyck. The theme was perhaps based on a comedy by Dancourt. Watteau always retained a taste for the theater, which he learned from Gillot, a painter of scenes from the *Commedia Italiana* and one of his first teachers, according to Caylus in his biography of Watteau.

Watteau painted with a light brush, as is particularly noticeable in the foliage, while the figures are drawn and emphasized with a slightly heavier touch

JEAN–BAPTISTE–SIMÉON CHARDIN. *Self-Portrait.*
One of Chardin's late works, the self-portrait is signed and dated 1775. The artist began to use pastels around 1770, when he was an old man. This picture shows no sign of senility, however; his delicate colors soften and modulate the shadows, while the areas struck by light are emphasized by fine white strokes. Although he is best known as a painter of still-lifes and bourgeois scenes, Chardin shows here his extraordinary ability as a portraitist through this frank and sensitive exploration of his own character. Refusing fine clothing and elegant poses, he wears the cap of a common man, as if in protest against all pretension. His introspective candor here and the honesty of his other works show his determination to be free of any preconceptions.

JEAN–BAPTISTE–SIMÉON CHARDIN. *Still-life with Pipe.* *p. 94*
Chardin's still-lifes were a complete novelty in 18th-century painting. He dedicated himself obstinately to this genre which the Academy despised, and which he had cultivated out of necessity, in painting screens and door panels. Diderot, one of Chardin's greatest supporters, wrote what is perhaps one of the best definition of his painting: "The magic of his work is difficult to grasp. He uses thick layers of color, one over the other, with the final effect filtering through from underneath.

ANTOINE WATTEAU
Valenciennes 1684–1721
*The Embarkation for Cythera*
(circa 1717)
Detail. Oil on canvas; 50″ × 75 1/2″.

JEAN–BAPTISTE SIMÉON CHARDIN
Paris 1699–1779
*Self-Portrait* (1775)
Pastel; 18″ × 15″

At times it looks as if a cloud of steam has blown across the canvas, at others as if light foam has been tossed at it . . . If you go close, everything becomes confused, flattens out, disappears; when you back off, the forms reappear and come to life."

JEAN–BAPTISTE SIMÉON CHARDIN
Paris 1699–1779
*Back from Market* (1739)
Oil on canvas; 18″ × 14 1/2″.

JEAN–BAPTISTE–SIMÉON CHARDIN. *Back from Market.*
*Back from Market* and other works by Chardin were exhibited at the Louvre Salon of 1739, and show us how Chardin had by that time created a style all his own, emphasizing domestic interiors, everyday objects, the middle class. In 1881, the Goncourts wrote "He limits his painting to the humble world to which he belongs, and to which belong his habits, his thoughts, his affections . . . he adheres to the illustration and representation of those scenes which touch him and which move him . . ." In the Louvre painting, Chardin treats his subject with a liberty which seems to foreshadow the realism of the 19th century. He worked outside the fashionable currents of his day, and actually belonged to the trend of French realism which persists from Le Nain to Courbet.

JEAN–BAPTISTE SIMEON CHARDIN
Paris 1699–1779
*Still-life with Pipe* (1760–63)
Oil on canvas; 12 1/2″ × 16 1/2″.

JEAN-HONORÉ FRAGONARD. *The Music Lesson.*

*The Music Lesson* appears to be a sketch rather than a finished picture. Fragonard's usually lively style is rather perfunctory in this work. A generation younger than Watteau, Boucher and Chardin, he was an unsuccessful pupil of the last. Subsequently he studied under Boucher, who at first made a great impression on him. In 1756 he won a Prix de Rome and went to Italy, where he studied Baroque painting and Pietro da Cortona in particular. From that time on his work became more animated and he developed a rapid, sure brilliant touch. He is the typical representative of the Rococo in France, even in his most conservative phase, and was deaf to the first notes of Neo-Classicism in the second half of the eighteenth century.

JEAN-HONORÉ FRAGONARD
Grasse 1732—Paris 1806
*The Music Lesson* (circa 1769)
Oil on canvas; 43 1/4″ × 47 1/4″.

# NINETEENTH CENTURY FRANCE

JACQUES-LOUIS DAVID. *Portrait of Madame Récamier.*
This painting belongs to David's high period, when he was the official painter to the Napoleonic age. It dates sixteen years after his famous *Oath of the Horatii* which was immediately recognized as a masterpiece with a message, an invitation to esthetic and political revolt, and later as one of the main documents of Neo-Classicism. By 1800 the revolutionary thrust of the new style was but a memory, and David's big mythological works, magnificent and brilliant as they may be, are considered by some critics to be overly doctrinaire. The portraits, on the other hand, remain among the highest products of his personality and style. The *Portrait of Madame Récamier* is one of the most significant, together with those of Count Potocki, the architect Desmaison, the Lavoisiers and the two magisterial self-portraits of 1790 and 1794. The delicate, soft figure—which offers a glimpse of what would be the fluid line of Ingres—turns a sensitive head toward the spectator. In the purity and sharpness of space (the tripod at the left is an important compositional element) there is a vibrant pictorial harmony, far removed from that "frigid execution" for which Delacroix reproached David. Note the touches of color on the cushions, on the gown, on the braided hair, scattered with quick glimpses of light.

JACQUES-LOUIS DAVID. *The Coronation of Napoleon.*
Immediately following the opening of the nineteenth century, David was commissioned by the Emperor to execute a number of large canvases to illustrate the major events of the time, including his own coronation. We know from documents that he was influenced by Rubens,

JACQUES-LOUIS DAVID
Paris 1748—Brussels 1825
*Portrait of Madame Recamier* (1800)
Oil on canvas; 59 × 94 1/2″.

JACQUES-LOUIS DAVID
Paris 1748—Brussels 1825
*The Coronation of Napoleon* (1805–1807)
Detail.
Oil on canvas; 240″ × 367″.
Signed and dated.

but it is also amply proved by the quality of the painting, which establishes an imposing synthesis of David's art and style. Our detail of the enormous composition furnishes additional evidence of David's genius as a portraitist. The head of the figure at the right certainly reminds us of his youthful passion for classical Roman sculpture.

EUGENE DELACROIX. *Liberty Leading the People.*
Like many of Delacroix's paintings, this one was inspired by a current political event, the 1830 insurrection of Paris. Almost to emphasize his enthusiasm as a liberal, the artist identified himself with the man brandishing a gun on the overturned barricade, while the armed mob is glimpsed through the smoke of the explosions that veil the city. (Six years earlier, Delacroix had painted, with parallel force, and on the same politically liberal theme, *Massacre of Chios,* inspired by the Greek struggle for independence.) Delacroix's rhetorical tone is compelling and the movements, the settings of the figures and, above all, the two bodies that almost completely dominate the foreground, reveal his emphasis on the theatrical. But the deep passion that motivated the artist more than redeems the violence of the scene. Two years later Delacroix made a long voyage to Morocco and Spain, a trip that proved crucial to his future.

EUGENE DELACROIX
Charenton-Saint-Maurice 1798—Paris 1863
*Liberty Leading the People* (1830)
Oil on canvas; 102 1/2″ × 128″; exhibited at the Salon of 1831, the painting was acquired by the French Government.

EUGENE DELACROIX. *Women of Algiers.*
"Here fame is a word without meaning: everything turns to a sweet laziness and it cannot be said that this is not the most desirable condition in the world." These words by Delacroix were written in a letter of 1832 from Tangier, and they explain the atmosphere of this masterpiece, deservedly among the most famous of the nineteenth century. It opens the long series of his paintings inspired by Oriental life, including lion hunts, Arabian horses, musicians and actors. The scene shows the interior of a harem, probably one visited by the artist during his African sojourn. It is evident that his first-hand observations left a deep mark, but above all they conditioned the development of his painting, as demonstrated in this luxurious setting where tiles, curtains, silks and jewels complement each other and yet each is painted with extraordinary precision. There is already a hint of that freedom of form which characterizes the later Delacroix, and of his complex compositional ideas which made him a rebel against the rules and doctrines of official art.

EUGENE DELACROIX
Charenton-Saint-Maurice 1798—Paris 1863
*Women of Algiers* (1834)
Oil on canvas; 71″ × 90″. Signed and dated. Exhibited at the Salon of 1834; bought by French Government for 3,000 francs.

JEAN–AUGUSTE–DOMINIQUE INGRES. *The Turkish Bath.*

*The Turkish Bath* was to have been the property of Prince Napoleon, but his wife considered the work immoral, so the Bonapartes bought a self-portrait instead. Ingres, after recovering the painting, altered the format to its circular shape and made a number of changes in the figures at the edges. Before coming to the Louvre, the painting was owned by the Turkish Ambassador to France and later by Prince Amédée de Broglie. Ingres had the theme of *The Turkish Bath* in mind for years. Jean Alazard has pointed out that in one of his notebooks the artist cites a few sentences from the letters of Lady Mary Wortley Montagu (published in 1764): "There were 200 women . . . The sofas were covered with cushions and rich carpets, on which sat the ladies, all being in the state of nature, that is, in plain English, stark naked . . . yet there was not the least wanton smile or immodest gesture among them." Ingres' *Bathers* of 1828 is an early statement of the idea. But

JEAN-AUGUSTE-DOMINIQUE INGRES
Montauban 1780—Paris 1867
*The Turkish Bath* (1826) Oil on canvas; diameter 41 1/2″—Signed and dated. Before entering the Louvre, it was owned by the Turkish Ambassador to Paris and later the Prince de Broglie.

the definitive version of *The Turkish Bath* dates from about 1860 and was finally finished in 1863, when the artist was 84. It can be considered his purest masterpiece; a sort of summation of the subject matter, content and problems he had treated many times before. The artist reveals himself, as always, conscious of the history of his own long artistic development. And it is extraordinary that none of this feeling of recapitulation detracts from the freshness of his inspiration. Many drawings show how specifically Ingres studied each figure, experimenting with them and visualizing them separately and in groups. The creative process was therefore long, and the power of abstract expression can be called absolute. The artist was completely immersed in his search for that depth and mastery of image to which he subordinated all other values. In this work are revealed some of his clearest and most daring intuitions, like that of "distorting" anatomy, and not losing himself in details, but forcing a central idea. The nude in the right foreground shows how Ingres found harmony in "deformation."

THEODORE GERICAULT. *The Raft of the Medusa,* (preliminary study). *The Raft of the Medusa* was to have been the first of a series of large paintings and was preceded by some 50 studies, of which this is probably one of the last. The studies have noticeable differences: missing in this one, for instance, are the body thrown overboard (foreground) and the dying man on the edge of the raft (left). Although incomplete, the composition of the central figures is already evident, and this sketch is considered by some authorities to be superior to the huge masterpiece that derives from it.

THEODORE GERICAULT. *The Raft of the Medusa.*
In 1816 Géricault, barely 25 years old, went to Italy, where he became fascinated with the works of the Classical and Renaissance masters. Upon his return to Paris in 1817, it was clear how deeply his visit to Italy had affected him when he undertook his most famous single canvas, *The Raft of the Medusa.* Many suggestions have been made as to which artists most influenced Géricault; from Michelangelo to Guercino, Gros to Prud'hon. B. Nicholson feels that a number of English and American painters of the late eighteenth century, especially Copley, left their impress on the artist. The *Raft*, according to Ragghianti, demonstrates the possibilities of "majestic historic continuity," without diminishing originality. In spite of its complex movements, intense passions and the gesticulations, violent foreshortenings of the limbs and bodies, the whole composition has a severe pyramidal structure that was roundly denounced by many contemporaries. Particularly objectionable were the shrouds (not shown in the sketch). The scene is foreshortened, receding swiftly to the horizon, but the vast dimensions of the canvas compel you to look and think, which was the intention of the artist who conceived of the painting as a "public"

THEODORE GERICAULT
Rouen 1791—Paris 1824
*The Raft of the Medusa* (1818)
Study. Oil and pen on canvas;
25 1/2" × 32 1/2".

THEODORE GERICAULT
Rouen 1791—Paris 1824
*The Raft of the Medusa* (1818–1819)
Oil on canvas; 193 1/2″ × 282″—Exhibited at the Salon of 1819, then in England for two years, the painting remained unsold until the artist died. Auctioned in November 1824, it was bought by Gericault's friend Dedreux-Dorcy, who a few months before had helped the dying artist.

message. Rejecting other episodes of the scandalous event (the shipwrecked seamen of the Medusa were set adrift on a raft in the Mediterranean and there were rumors of cannibalism), Géricault picked the moment when the survivors catch sight of the gunboat Argus that rescued them. Aside from the inevitable controversy it aroused in its time, the *Raft* immediately became famous, evoking enthusiastic praise from both critics and public.

CAMILLE COROT
Paris 1796—1875
*Souvenir of Mortefontaine* (1864)
Oil on canvas; 25 1/2″ × 35″.

CAMILLE COROT. *Souvenir of Mortefontaine.*
A look at Corot's major paintings makes *Souvenir of Mortefontaine* and similar works seem a bit sketchy and ordinary. But in any one of his masterly Italian scenes, bright French landscapes, portraits or figures, from the young nude of Mariette to the old *Woman at the Well* (Kröller-Müller Museum), you see an artist completely wrapped up in himself, completely oblivious to the life around him—artistic, social or political. Until about 1850 Corot's masterpieces were unknown: public recognition finally came to him through a series of large compositions. In this romantic *Souvenir,* the artist evokes the imaginative re-creation of an atmosphere which remembers the eighteenth century. Freshness catches your eye in the foreground touches of light, the transparency of the shadows, the delicacy of the background passages. A lofty tree dominates the rectangle and conceals most of the horizon, creating a mild effect of crosslighting, echoed in the small figures silhouetted against the clear, still waters.

FRANCOIS MILLET
Gruchy 1814—Barbizon 1875
*The Gleaners* (1848)
Oil on canvas; 21 1/4″ × 26″.

FRANÇOIS MILLET. *The Gleaners.*

*The Angelus,* 1859, and *The Gleaners,* 1857, continue to move the public today just as they did when they were executed. They are typical of the struggling Millet, who grew up on a farm in Normandy, and who, until he was almost 35, could not find his artistic direction. He hated the noise and frantic atmosphere of Paris and found a refuge in the little village of Barbizon in 1849. There he met, among other painters, Théodore Rousseau, whose friend he became. This was a happy and active time for Millet. He followed the style of rural Realism introduced in *The Gleaners,* especially in the three figures that stand out against the deep expanse of mowed fields. Note the firmness of the simple design, the absence of anecdote and details not essential to the dignity of the scene. The tiny figures in the background—wagon, horses, houses, trees, hay stacks—are an integral part of the wide landscape where man wears himself out in toil and suffering. In Millet's art, man is almost always in the center, and in this he distinguishes himself from his Barbizon friends, who were trying to understand "the language of the forest." It is indicative that, much later, van Gogh admired and copied Millet.

GUSTAVE COURBET. *The Artist's Studio.*

When this painting and his *Burial at Ornans* were rejected by the Universal Exposition of 1855, Courbet built his own "Pavilion of Realism," and organized an exhibition of 40 of his paintings. The detail illustrated here is the central section of the great composition in which he portrayed artists and writers sharing "the common action" for Realism. Also included are a proletarian and an Irishwoman. The symmetrical dignity of *Burial at Ornans* is a simply articulated scene, even though the figures are spread out across the composition. It can be called a synthesis of his cultural and formal experiences up to that time and in it we still find traces of his romantic and literary youth. His study of Velázquez and Ribera, of the seventeenth-century Dutch, of Caravaggio are evident in *The Studio;* yet all is converted to a style that separates Courbet from the past as well as from his contemporaries. The artist's strength and vitality hide but at the same time reveal his process of selection and comprehension, accomplished intelligently and with a precise purpose. Culture and a sense of reality—a passion for generous and fervid living—are united. Courbet was anything but "naive," ingenuous, or lacking in intellect; he would never submit to rules or participate in programs; he was a rebel, yet not without tenderness. We sense him here, too, in the figure of the child and in the nude who personifies Courbet's ideal woman. We see him in the entire group, and in the center, alone at his easel, in a world of illusion, but still close to the values and to the eternal allegories of life.

EDOUARD MANET. *Olympia.* *p. 110*

"The flesh tone is dirty, the model is nothing"; "This brunette is thoroughly ugly: her face is stupid, her skin cadaverous . . . all this clash of colors, of impossible shapes, is stupefying." These are two of the many negative opinions and "savage reviews" which appeared in Paris newspapers between May and June of 1865 (the first is by none other than the lapidary poet Théophile Gautier). Manet was hurt, as he was pained by the violence of visitors who wanted to attack the canvas itself. "Insults rain on me like hail," he wrote his friend the poet Baudelaire a short time later. And the malicious Degas, almost spitefully remarked, "Now you are as famous as Garibaldi!" It is difficult today when *Olympia* is considered one of the masterpieces of nineteenth-century painting to understand why it caused such a scandal and was so scorned. Robert Rey has noted that Manet rediscovered "a forgotten alphabet," and that it was his radical invocation of art history that was beyond the understanding of his contemporaries. *Olympia* lies on a silk shawl, resting on her right elbow, with raised head gazing at you, completely aloof. Her figure breathes light, and shadows frown subtly in the gray outlines. Her white flesh stands out vividly against the dark

GUSTAVE COURBET
Ornans 1819—La Tour-de-Peilz 1877
*The Artist's Studio* (1855)
Detail. Oil on canvas; 141 1/4" × 235 1/2". The work, together with *Burial at Ornans,* was rejected by the Universal Exposition of 1855. The artist then built his own shed, "Pavilion of Realism" in the center of Paris and there exhibited 40 of his paintings.

background from which emerges the pale gray-rose of the dress of the Negress bringing in a bouquet of flowers. *Olympia* represents, says critic Marangoni, "all Manet's aversion to the clever and superficial and is a challenge to the bad taste and spiritual baseness of the official painters and of the 'bourgeoisie.'" With exceptional simplicity, Manet accomplished his ideal of "a genuine vision pursued as far as brutality."

ÉDOUARD MANET. *The Balcony.*
Our detail reproduction is of the left-hand figure of a group of three leaning over the balcony, while a fourth is glimpsed inside a dimly lit room; she is Manet's friend, the painter Berthe Morisot. Her comment on the painting was that *The Balcony* had turned out "more strange than ugly." Like *Olympia,* it caused a minor scandal when it was exhibited. The detail, about actual size, reveals how intelligently the artist used quick, brilliant strokes to achieve his image.

EDOUARD MANET
Paris 1832–1883
*The Balcony* (1868)
Detail.
Oil on canvas; 65 7/8″ × 29 1/8″.

EDOUARD MANET
Paris 1832–1883
*Olympia* (1863)
Oil on canvas; 51″ × 74 3/4″. The work was shown at the 1865 Salon, and caused an unprecedented scandal. *Olympia* did not enter the Louvre until the beginning of this century.

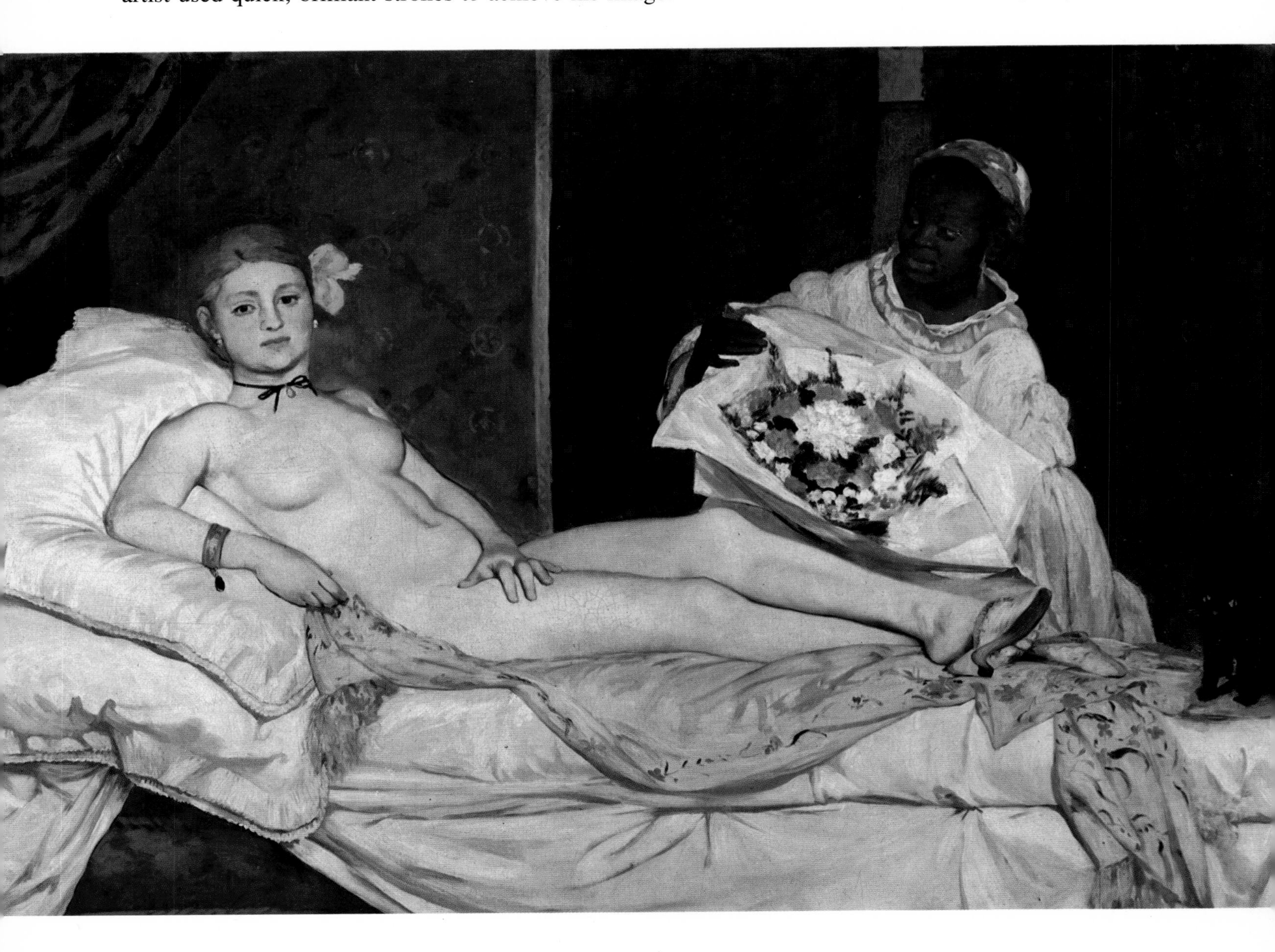

CAMILLE PISSARRO. *The Red Roofs.*

In 1874–75, at Pontoise, and then again in 1877, Pissarro and Cézanne worked side by side. It is almost certain that their close association and friendship contributed much to Pissarro's development, while Cézanne, on the other hand, recognized that he owed a good deal of his own growth to his older friend. This landscape is among the most representative of Pissarro's relationship with Cézanne between 1875 and 1880. With the help of Sisley and Monet, Pissarro, through selfless exertion, was mainly responsible for maintaining the cohesion of the Impressionist group and participated in all their shows from 1874 on. He had a sense for construction and felt that likenesses should develop slowly. Here you see, for example, his method of drawing with color, systematically superimposing dabs of color to create a mellow density and richness of tone. Émile Zola emphasized the "heroic simplicity" of Pissarro's art when he wrote: "It is enough to glimpse such works to understand that behind them is a man, an honest and vigorous personality, incapable of lying."

CLAUDE MONET. *Rouen Cathedral in Full Sunlight.*

During the winter months of 1892 and 1893, Claude Monet visited Rouen and, working with his characteristic energy, painted a series on the cathedral as he saw it from a window on the rue du Grand Pont at

CAMILLE PISSARRO
Saint-Thomas (Antilles) 1832—Paris 1903
*The Red Roofs* (1877)
Oil on canvas; 24 1/4″ × 25 1/2″.

CLAUDE MONET
Paris 1840—Giverny 1926
*Rouen Cathedral in Full Sunlight*
(1892–1893)
Oil on canvas; 42″ × 24 3/4″.

EDGAR DEGAS
Paris 1834–1917
*Two Laundresses* (circa 1884)
Oil on canvas; 30″ × 32 1/2″.

different hours of the day. Twenty of the 50 pictures, many of which he completed in his studio at Giverny, were exhibited in 1895 at Durand-Ruel's gallery. The cathedral's façade is always in the foreground and fills the whole rectangle. Light plays on the complex shapes, modifies and transposes the relationships between masses, continually altering the tones and local colors. Monet often complained of losing his youthful ability, of no longer being able to capture the fleeting instant, the momentary glimpse. But his Rouen Cathedral cycle comes closest to the modern vision, even if the happiest balance in Monet's art appears in the decade of 1870–80.

PIERRE-AUGUSTE RENOIR. *Moulin de la Galette.*
*Moulin de la Galette,* along with *The Luncheon of the Boating Party,* which he painted five years later, are shining examples of Renoir's genius, his innate talent for painting, his indifference to any form of intellectualism. Most interesting in this large composition, beautifully executed with an exact sense of space and with a marvellous impression of a crowd given by the superimposition of the faces, is the kaleidoscopic sparkling of color that filter unevenly through the leafy trees. The scene is lively. The daily life of Paris in the second half of the nineteenth century could not have found a more lyric and human interpreter. Rarely has painting made it possible to grasp so much of the contemporaneous poetic spirit.

EDGAR DEGAS. *Two Laundresses.*
The most commonplace, insignificant aspects of life and things attracted Edgar Degas, because for him they were the most suitable to "embody a clear vision." Here it is two laundresses at their daily work. What could have been a sketch of sorts, became under Degas' brush a wonderfully designed painting with rhythmic arrangements of contrasts and

PIERRE-AUGUSTE RENOIR
Limoges 1841–Cagnes 1919
*Moulin de la Galette* (1876)
Detail. Oil on canvas; 51 1/2″ × 69″.

HENRI RAYMOND DE TOULOUSE-LAUTREC
Albi 1864—Malrome 1901
*The Clowness Cha-U-Kao* (1895)
Gouache on board;
22 1/2″ × 16 1/2″.

dislocations of form. The most habitual, banal and private gestures are turned into admirable compositional instruments. A flat table establishes a downward diagonal movement opposing a movement from the opposite direction in the yawning figure. By such formal means and through Degas' rejection of any sentimentality about the laundress' sore arms, her bearing is presented in an absolute and dignified manner. The delicate, almost velvety color underlines the originality of one of the most coherent and forceful visions of any time.

RAYMOND HENRI DE TOULOUSE-LAUTREC. *The Clowness Cha-U-Kao.*

This is one of the most intense and vigorous paintings of Toulouse-Lautrec, whose best works were produced in the last ten years of the nineteenth century. The figure is almost monumental, and yet it has new motifs and forms and a new conception of space that shows the influence

PAUL CEZANNE
Aix-en-Provence 1839–1906
*The Card Players* (1890–92)
Oil on canvas; 17 3/4″ × 22 1/2″.

of Degas, whom Lautrec admired and who was his true teacher. The focal point is the yellow skirt that spirals around the heavy figure of the clowness. Despite her swelling, spilling form, she is invested with a stupendous energy, which depends on the quick impression, or what can be called the lightning-like style so unique to Lautrec. Notwithstanding the explosive passage of yellow, Lautrec was intolerant of "beautiful" painting and unwilling to go back and repaint what he had already done. Thus his corrections and deletions add to the total effect of the image.

PAUL CÉZANNE. *The Card Players.*
There are several studies and versions of this picture; one of them contains four figures, but this famous painting probably best reflects Cézanne's conception and his aspiration to solemnity. It reveals, among

other things, an exceptional composition, on a level with the best works of this great master. The symmetrical organization gains intensity from a use of delicate, sensitive variations on divided and related colors. The background in itself is a comment on the figures—it is completely harmonious but implies a different emotion. The controlling colors suggest a timeless dignity. Light, almost fluid, flows with sudden movements and vibrations that suggest an incisive, subtle handwriting. Cézanne continued to accent this more sensitive style in his later works, creating a cornerstone for modern art.

PAUL GAUGUIN
Paris 1848—Atuana (Marquesas Islands) 1903
*The White Horse* (1898)
Oil on canvas; 55 1/2″ × 35 3/4″.

PAUL GAUGUIN. *The White Horse.*
The taste and decorative instinct of Gauguin, and the new idea of color he evolved even before he went to Tahiti, are exemplified in this painting where he seems to overcome any and all programmatic esthetics. Here oranges, blues, reds, greens are used with a surprising liberty that later was to become the banner of the Fauves. The perspective he employed is based on the Japanese prints that had become known in Paris before Gauguin's Brittany period. Whether because of the way the horses moved, or because of the stream opening into the bottom of the picture, or because of the more broadly painted forms at the edges of the canvas, the total effect of the painting appears very personal. In such values as these are caught the contributions of a master who was erroneously judged as either savage or primitive by critics of the times.

VINCENT VAN GOGH. *Self-Portrait.*
Two months after finishing this masterpiece, Vincent van Gogh shot himself through the chest. His final letters expressed terror, then resignation. However, he worked incessantly up to the end. He painted landscapes and portraits, among them the magnificent one of the Impressionists' friend Dr. Gachet and this equally great self-portrait. His will and psychological insight and passionate concentration did not stop him from spreading rhythmic brushstrokes in tortuous waves on the canvas and into his torrential cascades of man, earth, sky. The background of this self-portrait could easily have been the sky that rose over the yellow fields of the Oise. From this background, which the jacket re-echoes and almost seems to turn into folds of cloth, Vincent's head boldly detaches itself, seemingly lost in the knowledge of his destiny.

*See p. 120*

VINCENT VAN GOGH
Groot Zundert 1853—Auvers-sur-Oise 1890
*Self-Portrait* (1890)
Oil on canvas; 25 3/5″ × 21 1/4″.

# ITALY

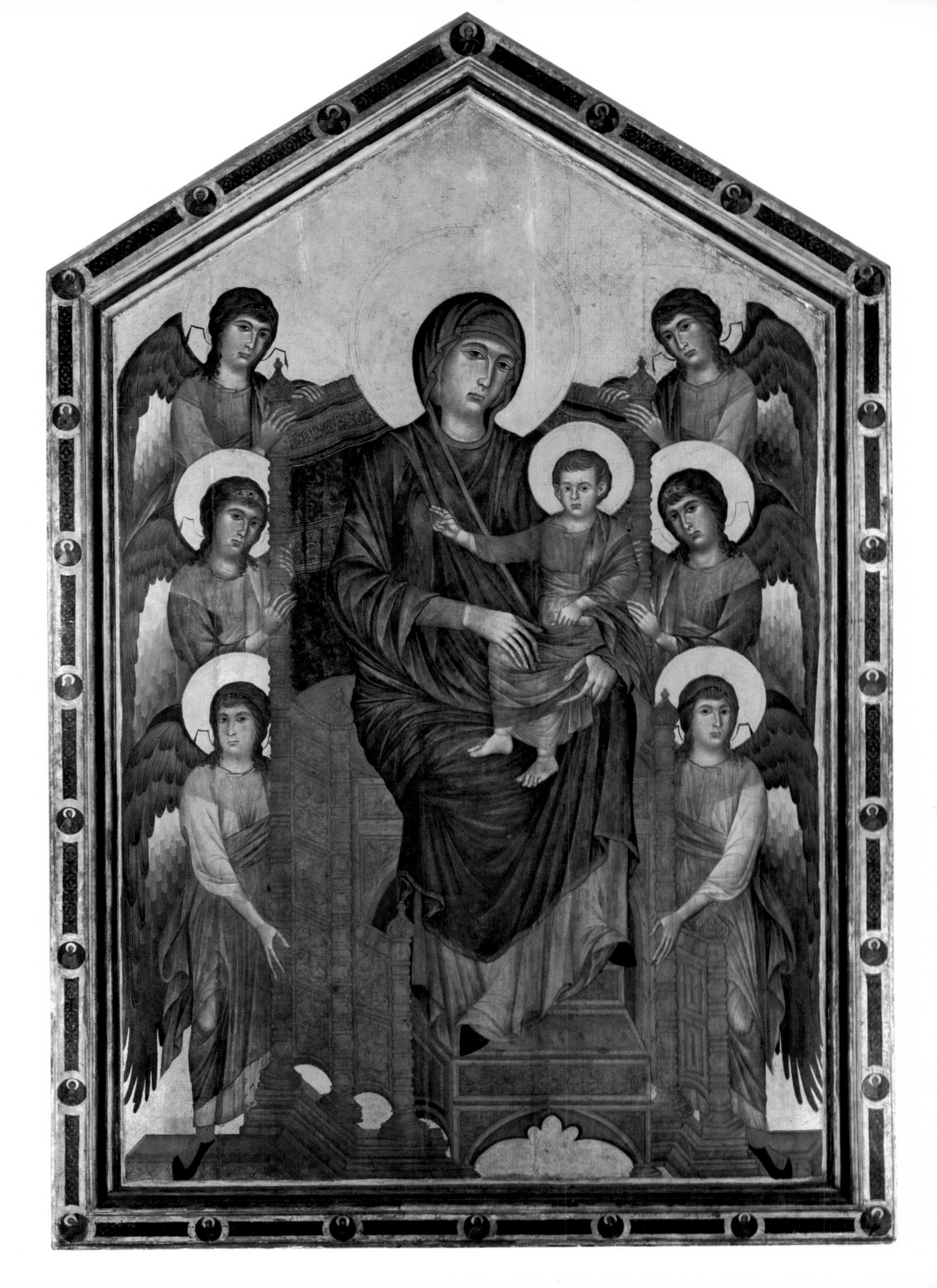

CIMABUE. *Madonna in Majesty.*

The painting was commissioned for the Church of St. Francis in Pisa; it remained there until the nineteenth century. The Virgin sits on a decorated throne set at a slant so that the line of her body follows that of the steps and the throne. Marking the planes in depth are the great golden nimbus inserted between her body and the back of the throne and the three pairs of angels set up against the throne to which their bodies and hook-like fingers cling in precise columnar arrangement.

The gold background here no longer serves as metallic curtain, screen or backdrop. It becomes real space. A limited space, to be sure, stretching out into a supernatural dimension: but nevertheless a space, structured by elements which subdivide it. Smaller areas are carefully blocked out, as for example the folds on the Virgin's sides, arms and knees. Her head is enclosed in an oval frame like those of Arnolfo di Cambio. After the tormented, ornamented linear style of the artist's *Christ* in Arezzo and the fantastic visions of the frescoes in Assisi (for example the *Crucifixion* where the medieval transcendental ideal still caused the works to vibrate with tensions and contrasts), Cimabue here seems to want to express himself in a more peaceful settled way. He avoids both the exalted and the dramatic style with its anxieties and high emotions. He seems to be attempting to communicate his own serene affirmation of faith to the visitors of the Church of St. Francis in Pisa.

CIMABUE
Florence 1240 (?)—Pisa 1302 (?)
*Madonna in Majesty* (1295–1300)
Tempera on panel; 167″ × 108 1/2″. Executed for the Church of St. Francis in Pisa, where it remained until 1882, when it was taken as part of Napoleon's booty.

SIMONE MARTINI. *Christ on the Road to Calvary.*

This small panel was once part of an altarpiece representing the *Passion of Christ* which is today divided between the Louvre and the Antwerp and Berlin museums. In spite of its size, the picture is extremely concentrated. Its structure is formed by the contrast between the geometric, block-like shape of the city, seen in perspective from the lower left, and the mob accompanying Christ. This brightly-colored group, irregularly subdivided, comes down from above, almost bursting forth from the narrow opening, then bearing to the right so that the rapid upward movement is braked and interrupted. The space, both within the walls and outside, is airless. The slope is lighted only in the background, where the figure of Christ with his bright red mantle carrying the Cross forms the focus of the composition. Such a composition, intensely personal and not to be translated into "normal" objective dimensions, expresses the sure style of Simone Martini, who matches in his painting the aims and literary achievements of his friend Petrarch. Both artists were conscious of taking part in an enormously creative period of European civilization, and indeed, Simone Martini was himself responsible for many elements of one of its most successful creations, the so-called "International Gothic" style.

SIMONE MARTINI
Siena 1284 (?)—Avignon 1344
*Christ on the Road to Calvary* (1335–40)
Tempera on panel; 9 1/2″ × 6 1/4″.
This small panel was once part of an altarpiece depicting the *Passion* of Christ. Other panels, representing *the Archangel Gabriel, The Annunciation, The Crucifixion* and *The Deposition* are in the Antwerp Museum, while *The Entombment* is in the Berlin Museum.

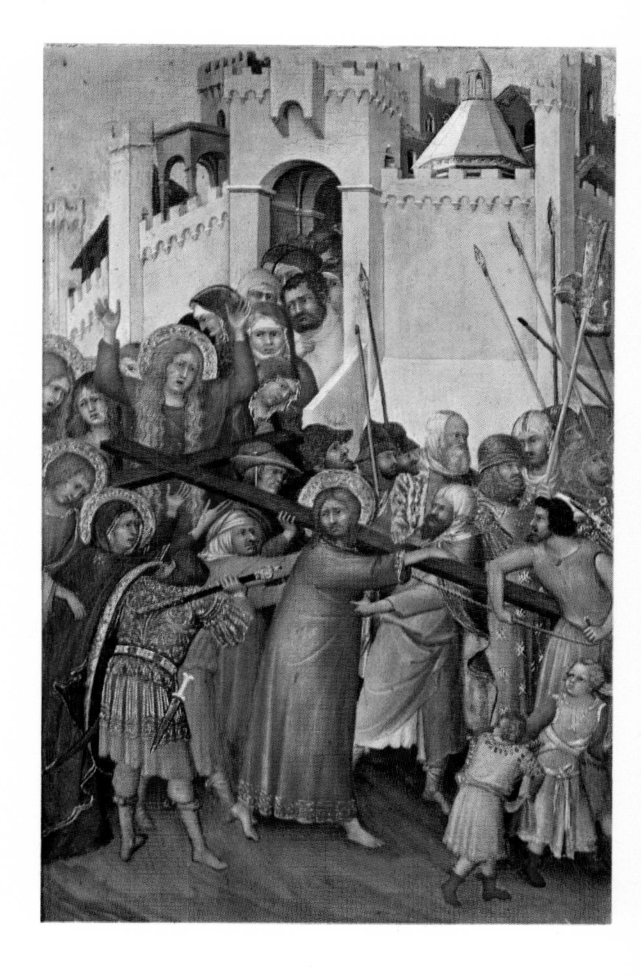

PISANELLO. *Portrait of a Princess of the House of Este.*
The princess is either Margherita Gonzaga, wife of Lionello d'Este, or Ginevra d'Este, wife of the notorious Sigismondo Malatesta. She wears on her sleeve the arms of the Este family, a vase or amphora. Her portrait is an example of Pisanello's intellectual style, of his aristocratic avoidance of the natural in favor of the sophisticated taste of the courtly world within which he moved so gracefully. His painting portrays acutely, often sympathetically, characteristic motifs from this world: animals in gardens or at the hunt, for instance, or the fashionable dress and decorations of lords and ladies. Here he shows the lady with every hair painstakingly, remorselessly drawn back, tightly bound by a ribbon. Her bosom is forced in a rigid bodice. Far from hiding the weakness of the profile, he emphasizes the roundness of the forehead and the bare neck. This delicate, vulnerable, asexual nakedness fits into a background of flowers and butterflies, represented like so many crystals and precious stones. As her skin and dress are transformed into marble, so, too, the sky is changed into lapis-lazuli by the artist's marvelous alchemy.

PAOLO UCCELLO. *The Rout of San Romano.* *p. 126*
Paolo Uccello painted, in three panels, the battle fought in June 1432 near San Romano by the Florentine and Sienese armies under the *"condottieri"* Niccolò da Tolentino, Micheletto Attendolo da Cotignola on one side, and Bernardino della Carnia on the other. Today the panels are divided among the Uffizi Gallery in Florence, the National Gallery in London and the Louvre. Neither side is favored by the artist: the victorious Florentines cannot be distinguished from the losing Sienese. We have an immobile, enclosed, complex composition of white, bluish brown and rose-toned horses champing at the bit and stamping their powerful hoofs, horsemen shut into the shining anonymity of their silver-painted steel armor, and an intricate pattern of clubs, lances and pennants. Each element is reduced to a blind and splendid instrument of death. The artist, avoiding narration, created a kind of mysterious and frighteningly still masquerade, with all the figures caught in the instant just before the final catastrophe.

*p. 127*
DOMENICO GHIRLANDAIO. *Francesco Sassetti with His Grandson.*
Ghirlandaio, who often showed an interest in factual description, executed portraits in one of two ways. Most frequent is the type emphasizing learned allusions and details of dress which result in an "official" identification of a person. At times, however, as here, he concentrated on emotional relationships which allowed him to reveal the inner character of the people involved. In this painting of the famous Florentine banker Francesco Sassetti, Ghirlandaio is less concerned with his position in society than with the vigor and robustness of his old age, with all its faults, such as the growth on his large nose. Most important is the way in which the old man reacts to his grandson, who moves affectionately toward him. This relationship is echoed in the red color of the old man's dress, repeated in the boy's hat and jacket as though to underline the intimate relationship and continuity of these two, the oldest and youngest members of the family.

PISANELLO
Verona (?) c. 1395—Verona 1455
*Portrait of a Princess of the House of Este*
(1435–40) Tempera on panel; 17″ × 11 3/4″.

*Above:*

DOMENICO GHIRLANDAIO
Florence 1449—Florence 1494
*Portrait of Francesco Sassetti with His Grandson* (circa 1490)
Tempera on canvas; 24 1/2″ × 18″.

*Right:*

ALESSIO BALDOVINETTI
Florence 1425—Florence 1499
*Madonna and Child* (1450–55)
Tempera on panel; 41″ × 30″.

*Left:*

PAOLO UCCELLO
Florence 1397—Florence 1475
*The Rout of San Romano* (1456–60)
Detail. Tempera on panel; 71 1/2″ × 124 3/4″. The battle was represented on three separate panels, which are today divided among the Louvre, the Uffizi Gallery, Florence, and the National Gallery, London. The series decorated a hall on the first floor of the Medici Palance in Florence on the via Larga, along with other paintings which are lost, two by Paolo Uccello and one by Pesellino.

ALESSIO BALDOVINETTI. *Madonna and Child.*
The artist's goal seems to have been to co-ordinate the structural elements of the composition in space through a use of perspective of color rather than of geometric lines, in a way already worked out by Domenico Veneziano. With this ideal in mind, he enlarged certain areas and reduced others, forming the surface into an irregularly articulated whole over which plays the diffused cold, early-morning sun, alternately creating areas of light and shadow. In accordance with this system, the halo is not shown as a line, but as a large mirror-like disk; the child is like a wax model whose cylindrical volume is emphasized by the ribbon-like band tied around his waist; the pillow marks the depth of the balustrade; and the Virgin holds her hands before her in an opposed direction from that of the arms of the chair, thus emphasizing the space before her, which balances the space which extends behind her in the sloping, deserted landscape. Such a static composition brings out the precious quality of all colors and textures, such as the delicacy of veils and velvets, of ivory-colored skin, shiny metallic cloths and variegated marble.

ANDREA MANTEGNA. *Parnassus.*

*Parnassus,* the traditional title for this work, is today recognized to be based on an erroneous interpretation of the painting. Scholars have repeatedly attempted, without ever agreeing, to work out the iconography of this painting and of the other four pictures of a group painted by Mantegna and Perugino, then at the height of their careers, and Lorenzo Costa, for Isabella of Este's *studiolo* around the end of the fifteenth century. The subject was chosen by the learned Isabella and her intellectual humanist friends. In any case, this work is of interest as an example of Mantegna's purist "classical" style, a style which often coexists with his other complex and heroic manners. Here we can clearly distinguish the three sections of the composition: Vulcan pointing towards Venus and Mars, shown serenely embracing each other; the women dancing, accompanied by Orpheus; and, finally, the enigmatic couple on the right. Tying these three elements together are the spaces and the converging and parallel lines of the limbs of the figures, the floating scarves, the lances, rocks and foliage. Such a clear sym-

ANDREA MANTEGNA
Isola di Cartura 1431—Mantua 1506
*Parnassus* (1495–97)
Tempera on canvas; 63″ × 75 1/2″. In the Louvre are also the three paintings of the *Myth of Comus,* by Mantegna and Lorenzo Costa, Costa's *Allegory* and Perugino's *Triumph of Chastity,* all painted like *Parnassus,* for the study of Isabella d'Este in her palace at Mantua.

PIETRO PERUGINO
Citta della Pieve 1445—Fontignano 1524
*Apollo and Marsyas* (1490–1500)
Oil on panel; 15 1/4″ × 11 1/2″.

metry, both in depth and on the plane, exemplifies that classical tradition which would continue from Poussin to Ingres.

PIETRO PERUGINO. *Apollo and Marsyas.*
Art historians have not always appreciated the importance of the inner structure of Perugino's altarpieces. But such works as this, in which the human figure is freed from the conventional restrictions of "official" painting, have always been popular with critics and public alike. The figure becomes a part of the landscape, and enters into close relationship with trees, rivers, hills, streets and castles. The relationship is an unexpected one, however. On the one hand, nature is relaxed; humanized and good-natured, but not completely taken over by cultivation. On the other hand, in a kind of contrast, the forms of Apollo and Marsyas are carefully and consciously modeled and controlled. Marsyas appears neither as satyr nor hairy shepherd, but as a handsome, polished youth. Their fixed poses which form the backbone of the composition are regulated according to an intellectual ideal, a mathematical, musical harmony.

LEONARDO DA VINCI (?). *The Annunciation.*
Critics have repeatedly discussed the problem of this picture's attribution: is it by Leonardo or Lorenzo di Credi? In favor of Leonardo are the complex levels of meaning, the character of the brushstroke and the sure touch of color relationships, with reddish-brown tones prevailing. In favor of a different attribution, however, is the manner in which areas are defined, the painstaking divisions between garden, neighboring lawns, path and corner of the wall, as well as the rigorous symmetry of the plane within which the two figures have been placed in a curved composition. The lack of care given to details and dress also points to someone other than Leonardo, possibly Lorenzo di Credi, who had studied with Leonardo under Verrocchio.

LEONARDO DA VINCI
Vinci 1452—Amboise 1519
*Portrait of Mona Lisa* (circa 1505)
Oil on panel; 30 1/4″ × 20 3/4″.

LEONARDO DA VINCI. *Portrait of Mona Lisa (La Gioconda).*
The surface of the picture has suffered from overpainting. The paint has oxidized and today we see the figure through a greenish haze, completely altering the original colors. The significance of the figure, too, has suffered from over-interpretation and false interpretations. Yet somehow the Mona Lisa has, almost miraculously, survived all these vicissitudes. Its meaning is not easy to understand; but neither is it impenetrable, if one studies Leonardo's figurative motifs in the context of his scientific interests. In painting the Mona Lisa, Leonardo was reacting against a fifteenth-century concept of space which, after having been the focus of scientific and esthetic investigation during the whole of the century, was tied to a rigid Aristotelian classification. He has swept aside the traditional division of the horizontal plane by converging radial lines and the subordination of the single elements to a single vanishing point, and substituted, in their stead, a gradation of light and color. The frame no longer limits the figure; even the wooden panel loses its solidity. The viewer finds himself before an open window, as Alberti said, or as Leonardo himself put it, "a glass wall"; just beyond is the figure, placed in three-quarter profile, with hands together, the arm of the chair at a slant. There is movement in the evanescent, crinkly folds of the dress, the veil, the hair. A barely perceptible smile touches the curve of the mouth and the eyelids. Everything breathes and trembles imperceptibly: the waves of the water, the mist, the clouds, even the scaly rocks in the infinite, vaporous landscape.

LEONARDO DA VINCI (?)
*The Annunciation* (1480–85)
Tempera on panel; 5 1/2″ × 28 3/4″. It was originally the central panel of an altarpiece representing a "Sacred Conversation," executed by Lorenzo di Credi, in the Cathedral of Pistoia.

RAPHAEL. *Madonna and Child and St. John The Baptist.*
This is perhaps the work which best reveals the influence on Raphael of Leonardo's mature work, as represented, for example, by the Louvre cartoon for *St. Anne.* Raphael painted this *Madonna* during his stay in Florence, in 1504–09. He deliberately chose certain Leonardesque motifs, and discarded others. Leonardo fragments matter and brings movements into it in an attempt to represent the dynamic aspect of the cosmos, with its infinite possibilities for transformation; Raphael insists instead on a clearly defined articulation of objects represented in their immutable, crystalline interrelationships. This is why the fluid, descending pyramidal structure of Leonardo's *St. Anne,* which was the pattern Raphael was following, is here completely changed. The resplendent colors form a measured, clear space. Within this space the lines of limbs and garments, uninterrupted by jewels or other decorative motifs, form a clear pattern.

RAPHAEL
Urbino 1483—Rome 1520
*Madonna and Child and St. John the Baptist*
(1507) Oil on panel 48″ × 31 1/2″. The work is signed and dated; it can be identified with a *Madonna* which Vasari says Raphael painted in Florence for Filippo Sergardi.

RAPHAEL. *Portrait of Baldassarre Castiglione.*
The structure of the figure is not only pyramidal, but almost prismatic, worked out in depth. This prism leads the eye from the hands at the lower left, along the diagonal lines of the forearms to the elbows, and from there in depth, back from each of the successive levels outlined in turn by fold, shoulder and collar. The solid frame of the body is emphasized with its wide shoulders and deep chest. Above it, the face

RAPHAEL
*Portrait of Baldassarre Castiglione* (1515–16)
Oil on panel, transferred to canvas;
29 1/2″ × 25 1/2″.

stands out, reflecting the whiteness of the shirt, and framed by the brim of the wide hat, whose dark outline adds to the stability of the form. The artist here is deeply interested in the character of his subject, the author of a famous book of manners, *The Courtier*. He seems, indeed, to be translating Castiglione's intellectual and moral character into pictorial terms by means of three-dimensional geometric, architectural forms, covered with luxurious furs and velvets in greenish yellows and browns.

GIORGIONE. *The Concert*.
The attribution of this work has been the subject of spirited debate: today the chief competitors are Giorgione and Titian. The painting's most striking quality is the stillness and isolation of the figures. There seems to be no communication between them, and one is aware of the fixity of their gazes. The nude about to fill the pitcher at the fountain bends forward languidly in precarious balance, her thoughts far removed from the present movement. As she turns she shows, only momentarily and incompletely, her naked flank; her breasts are hidden by the curve of her arm. What a world of difference there is between the classical model of this figure, doubtless a statue like the Venus of Milos, and this pictorial rendering, all lights and shadows, the solid forms lost in the brightly lit folds of the drapery which is just barely held in place by the knees. Within the soft curve of the landscape can almost be heard the sound of the lute, the breathing of human figures and flocks, the rustle of leaves and of the grasses. It is late afternoon; as in some of Virgil's poems, the artist tries to recapture the nostalgic moods and movements of nature at sunset. Yet the consciously intellectual sophistication of the Renaissance man is clearly shown by the studied harmony of silks and velvets, contrasting with the magnificent naked forms of the women. Is this Giorgione, or Titian painting like Giorgione? The intensity and rhythm of the whole work speak in favor of its attribution to Giorgione.

GIORGIONE
Castelfranco 1477 (?)—Venice 1510
*The Concert* (1505–10)
Oil on canvas; 43 1/4″ × 54 1/4″.

TITIAN. *Man with a Glove.*
Already in this work, one of his earliest portraits, Titian shows his originality. The placement of the figure is typical of the artist. The figure is seen to the waist. The body is simply formed, included within repeated angles—the bent arm, the crossed leg. A few bright spots attract the eye: the open hand, laid easily on the lap, the opening of the jacket revealing the white cloth of the shirt, the clear-cut line of the nose. The youth who commissioned the portrait belonged no doubt to the upper classes of the Venetian Republic, perhaps even to the narrow circle of its ruling aristocracy. He sits quietly but not stiffly, looking at something we cannot see. The glove he holds, expensive, but soft and wrinkled from daily use, has rightly been chosen to characterize him. It tells us more about this anonymous young man and his place in society than do either the narrow, carelessly fluttering lace borders or the gold chain almost hidden on his chest. The focus of the whole picture leads to this glove, by the downward direction of the lighted features, the sloping lines of the shoulders and the pointing fingers.

TITIAN
Pieve di Cadore 1477 (?)—Venice 1576
*Portrait of an Unknown Gentleman, Man with a Glove* (circa 1510)
Oil on canvas; 39 1/4″ × 34 1/4″.

TITIAN. *Woman at the Mirror.*
The woman has been identified as either Titian's mistress or Laura Dianti, mistress of Alfonso d'Este. She was certainly Titian's favorite model and appears in his pictures again and again, probably not for

TITIAN
*Woman at the Mirror* (circa 1515)
Oil on canvas; 37 3/4″ × 30″.

sentimental reasons, but rather because her physical type was well adapted to his style. The broad, fluid planes of her face and shoulders allowed him to express those gradations of tone which were his specialty. Her crisply curled hair could reflect the light either in bright sparkling spots or in luminous waves. Over her broad breasts he could widen the neckline of the finely pleated blouse and, under her rounded arms, form deep shadows in the openings of the sleeves. The figure of the model here provides the focus for an intricate, irregular rhythm of concentric forms, starting from the surface of the head of her lover, who adjusts the mirror, leaning over the girl. Her gaze turns elsewhere; and the rhythm is then taken up by the forms of her body and dress: the neckline of her blouse, slipping off her shoulders, the rounded forms within the open bodice, and the diagonal *contrapposto* of her arms, as she turns to adjust her hair, while the other arm closes off the composition on the right, the hand resting on the solid form of the little vase.

TITIAN
*Deposition* (circa 1525)
Oil on canvas; 58 1/4″ × 88 1/2″. This is the first of a series of works commissioned by the Marquis of Mantua, Federico Gonzaga, nephew of Alfonso d'Este.

TITIAN. *Deposition.*
The influence of Michelangelo is visible in the weight of the bodies and in the opposition of forces in the foreground, as well as the sweeping movement with which Mary Magdalen supports the weeping Virgin.

This influence also explains the powerful frame of the body of Christ, hidden in the shadows except for the bony hands and pointed knees. Nevertheless, the artist, who is conscious of this influence, turns it to new uses. The essential structure is, to be sure, sculptural; a central group based on a solid human form. Tensions resulting from its insertion in an architectural composition, however, are exploited by the painter, who is here showing the Deposition not directly, as something which is being re-lived in the present, but rather as a reenacted scene. Even the artist's own emotional participation is overwhelmed by the epic proportions of the drama and by the splendid colors—golden reds, blues and yellows—lit by the dark splendor of a stormy twilight.

PAOLO VERONESE. *The Wedding at Cana.*
Veronese liked the theme of the banquet or supper. Many of his pictures show this motif, the best-known being the famous *Feast in the*

PAOLO VERONESE
Verona 1528—Venice 1588
*The Wedding at Cana* (1562–64)
Detail. Oil on canvas; 259 3/4″ × 389 3/4″.
Painted for the Refectory of the Convent of S. Giorgio Maggiore, Venice.

*House of Levi* in the Accademia, Venice. He always transformed the theme, setting the various episodes of the religious story into the luxurious surroundings of sixteenth-century Venice, with its colorful, cosmopolitan crowds of lords and ladies, servants, buffoons, exotic animals and pets, precious silverware and plate, embroidered tablecloths, all within architectural frames—colonnaded porticos, staircases, terraces—triumphantly open to the light of day. The background is Venice, with marble palaces reminiscent of the local architectural tradition following Coducci, and also of the contemporary classical architecture of Andrea Palladio.

It is within such a context that we must look at this painting. It has been compared unfavorably to other works of the artist, especially to his *Feast in the House of Levi*. It is true that the *Marriage at Cana* is less grandiose compressed as it is between the two rows of huge columns. There are too many different types of guests—Venetians, Turks,

Easterners, variously identified by their dress and features—of servants, musicians and paraphernalia in general. Yet the painting is of interest precisely for its experimental quality. It marks a moment of change, after which Veronese expressed himself in a different way, extending the use of quiet, white architectural frames to contrast with the bright colors of human figures.

JACOPO TINTORETTO. *Paradise.*
The subject is similar to that of the huge canvas painted for the Great Council Hall in the Doge's Palace in 1590. This smaller work cannot, however, be considered to be a sketch for the mural: at least it is not its preparatory study. Certain differences in style show that it probably should be dated 30 years earlier, to coincide with Tintoretto's work in the church of the Madonna dell'Orto. Perhaps it was a project for a commission which was never carried out, or perhaps the artist simply painted it for himself. The latter seems probable in view of the free flowing style. Groups of saints and of the blessed are placed within the rolling hemicycles, illuminated by a great light. We watch from below, while above, at a dizzying height, in the center of the "mystic rose," Christ is crowning the Virgin. In the "petals" of the rose all is transformed by color: clouds, figures and drapery are expressed in rapid strokes which define neither by outline nor by shadow, but by bright touches of gold on the rose and red colors, on the greens, above all on the predominant light blue and white. Tintoretto, who never pays too much attention to the solidity of his forms, here surpasses himself in the imaginative, fantastic reconstruction of the heavenly crowds, where any corporeal reality is denied and destroyed. All plastic values evaporate in this world where the successive widening of the "eternal circles" extends to the infinity of time and space.

JACOPO TINTORETTO
Venice 1518 (?)—Venice 1594
*Paradise* (1565–70)
Detail of left side.
Oil on canvas; 56 1/4″ × 14 1/2″.
Subject and composition are similar to that of the huge *Paradise* painted by Tintoretto in 1590 for the Great Council Hall of the Doge's Palace in Venice, but scholars agree this work is some twenty years earlier.

MICHELANGELO. *Bound Slave.* *p. 142*
The figure was executed for the base of the Tomb of Pope Julius II, an ambitious project, several times interrupted and reduced in scale by those who had commissioned the work. Michelangelo struggled with it for forty years. It was never completed; but the magnificent figures of the *Bound Slaves* bear witness to the incredible effort, both intellectual and physical, which Michelangelo expended upon it. It is in these figures that we can see the concentration he put into this work and the sense of commitment with which he carried it out. In fact, it is just in this instant when he applies himself to hew the human form out of the raw block of marble that we can sense the basic theme of his creative process. The long, almost serpentine, sinuous figure is blocked out by three angles—the elbows, and the knee bent forward, expressing extension in height,

width and depth. The figure suffers, in a long, slow spasm, constrained as it is by tight bonds and almost, it would seem, by the unyielding marble itself. Yet the artist in effect has conquered the material, transforming it by means of subtle modeling, lovingly emphasizing the swelling forms of the muscles, and achieving thereby luminous effects reminiscent of Praxiteles.

CORREGGIO. *Antiope.*
This composition was designed to be the first of a series of paintings representing the loves of Jupiter; others include the stories of Danaë, Leda, Io and Ganymede. The god, shown here in the form of a satyr, sees Antiope sleeping, with Eros at her side; he stops to admire her, lifting the drapery which covered her body. The painting is an excellent example of the artist's mature style. To his interest in Giorgione, an influence which reached him originally by way of Dosso Dossi, has been added the influence of Leonardo da Vinci. He adopts the results of Leonardo's style without accepting its origin, Leonardo's interest in the relationship between science and painting. Correggio uses the smoky tones of Leonardo, but uses them to enrich the sentimental, nostalgic, bucolic mood of the idyll. The forms are daringly foreshortened, curved in soft lines which lead to the face of Antiope. These lines are not constructed on an abstract, geometric pattern: they expand, they flow out of an open, asymmetric space, and run diagonally along the grassy slope. The group has been caught in an instant of immobility; but the figures already seem to glow with desire and the sensuous movement of dreams. Almost magically, they seem to have been called forth, out of the dark shadows of the forest, by the warm afternoon light. This light casts a golden glow on the flesh tones, and is reflected by the bright hair and by the flame of the thyrsus; at the same time it further dematerializes the already delicate grass, the spotted animal tail used as a quiver, and the lion skin on which is lying the little winged Eros.

BENVENUTO CELLINI. *The Nymph of Fontainebleau.* *p. 144*
Cellini went to France in 1540, invited by Francis I. He could not have found a climate more favorable to his tastes than the School of Fontainebleau. There Rosso Fiorentino together with Primaticcio and others were giving a new impetus to the local school; their taste, as a result of both classical and of persistent late Gothic influence, ran to imaginative, sometimes deformed or grotesque forms. It is in such an ambience that we can understand the elongated silhouette of the Nymph, with crescent-shaped forms echoing each other across the bronze plaque: the curved border of the mantle and the curve of the stag's horns. The decorative quality of the background—thickly dotted with animals, flowers, leaves, fruits and waving water transformed into a soft resting-place—can only be explained within this same context in which spatial problems were sacrificed to decoration.

MICHELANGELO
Caprese 1475—Rome 1564
*Bound Slave* (circa 1513)
Marble sculpture; 90 1/4″ high. Originally planned for the base of the Tomb of Pope Julius II. It was given by the artist to Roberto Strozzi, then living as an exile in France, along with the other *Slave* in the Louvre, at the time of one of the numerous interruptions and changes in the Pope's monument.

CORREGGIO (ANTONIO ALLEGRI)
Correggio 1489—Correggio 1534
*Antiope* (1524–25)
Oil on canvas; 74 3/4″ × 48 3/4″.
This is the first of a series of paintings representing the *Loves of Jupiter,* apparently executed for Federico Gonzaga, who planned to present them as a gift to Charles V.

BENVENUTO CELLINI
Florence 1500—Florence 1571
*The Nymph of Fontainebleau* (1543–44)
Bronze relief; 80 3/4″ × 161″.

ROSSO FIORENTINO
Florence 1495—Paris 1540
*Pietà* (1537–40)
Oil on panel, transferred to canvas;
62 1/2″ × 96 1/2″

ROSSO FIORENTINO. *Pietà.*
The work, executed for Anne de Montmorency, is one of the few surviving documents of the artist's activity in France between 1530 and 1540, when he was painter to the king and in charge of the decoration of the palace at Fontainebleau. It has been criticized for its excessively formal tone and for the absence of that artistic rebellion which characterizes the paintings he did in Tuscany and Umbria. There, he had made it a point to avoid traditional motifs, and had reacted against the "classical" Florentine manner, especially that of Andrea del Sarto. But these criticisms are unjust: the *Pietà* is actually a product of the artist's mature style, when he is no longer rebelling, and when even the influence of Michaelangelo, which in his youth he had over-emphasized, has now been absorbed more quietly and on a deeper level.

The figures are closely bound together within a rocky hollow, the edges of which are barely suggested by a jagged border. The forms of limbs and bodies, touched by the light, determine an asymmetric composition within a narrow frame. The eye moves along the wavering form of St. John, tightly enclosed within sheets of yellow and reddish color, and stops at the head of the Saint, prematurely grey, with its thick heavy locks. This form is included within the double diagonals formed by the livid body of Christ on the swelling, red pillow, and the open arms of the Virgin, who, like the figure beside her, is thickly wrapped in a purplish brown mantle. The diagonal opens, scissors-like, to contain Mary Magdalen: her form, advancing towards the foreground, is made up of broken folds, flesh and thick hair, over which there plays an ever-changing pattern of rose, yellow, green and wine-dark colors.

CARAVAGGIO. *The Fortune-Teller.* *p. 146*
According to tradition, this is one of the first paintings of Caravaggio executed in Rome. It is said, indeed, to be the one he painted to demonstrate his own anti-Academic bent, when he was advised to study Classical models. "He called in a gypsy who happened to be passing by in the street and painted her as she was telling the future . . . He also painted a young man with his gloved hand on his sword, holding out toward her

HIERONYMUS BOSCH
's Hertogenbosch circa 1450—circa 1516
*The Ship of Fools* (circa 1490)
Panel; 22 3/4" × 12 3/4". The motif of folly is here represented by the shipful of merry-makers —a motif quite common, especially in literature, in the 15th century—and connected to contemporary satire on the corruption of the clergy (indicated by the monk and the nun).

QUENTIN METSYS
Louvain 1466—Antwerp 1530
*The Moneychanger and His Wife* (1514)
Panel; 28" × 26 3/4". Signed and dated, "Quinten matsyss schilder 1514." This is doubtless the signed original which was the model for an enormous series of replicas and copies. It restates a convention, current in 15th-century Flemish painting, and became widely used in treating this popular theme.

PETER PAUL RUBENS. *The Arrival of Marie de' Medici at Marseilles.*
In spite of the enormity of the task and the speed of its execution, the entire series celebrating the Queen is from the artist's own hand; so, too, are the sketches, most of which are in Munich. Only minor help from assistants could have been contributed towards the final completion of the paintings. In this picture of the young Queen's disembarkation on French soil, Rubens has clearly divided the story into two horizontal zones, marked off by the diagonal line of the gangplank connecting the ship's deck with the not yet visible shore. Above, in the background—composed of fluctuating and intersecting decorative elements—can be seen foreshortened, the group of ladies-in-waiting and attendant mythological subjects, their figures softened by the pearly glow of the delicate colors and made even more lyrical by the rhythmic pattern of their gestures. The main episode below has far more emphasis. Rubens has used the mythological group of sea-divinities emerging from the glassy waves of an impossible sea, to realize one of the most daring, remarkable compositions of his career. We see bursting forth opulent naked forms, intertwined in incredible contortions, hurled forward by agitated waves of violent rhythms, of blazing colors occasionally frozen in sudden crystal light. The ornate, shining section of the ship on the left connects the two scenes with a solid, vertical movement. The immobile, static figure of the gentleman on deck, aloof from both action and participation in the scene, is almost a personification or symbol of detachment from any kind of engagement and of the emotional and formal control the artist, apparently so magnificently spontaneous and impulsive, constantly exercises in his paintings.

REMBRANDT VAN RIHN. *The Supper at Emmaus.* *p. 154*
The architectural setting of the composition, bare but monumental, with its few elements—the door, the engaged pillars, the niche framing and symbolically containing Christ—at once forms the background and suggests its structure, based on an internal diagonal axis moving from the foreground on the right towards the back on the opposite side. The figures gathered around the table form a vertical diagonal pattern which is varied internally by triangular patterns on the surface and in depth. This constant interplay of converging and diverging directions, of parallels and contrasts, is so skillfully carried out as to be noticed only by careful observation. The figure of Christ, the spiritual center, is the source of the light which radiates forth, resulting in sudden, daring illuminations of the faces and the hands of the pilgrims, permeating the surrounding darkness with soft evocative light and creating a climate of imaginative thoughtfulness, mysterious and solemn at the same time. The extreme simplicity of the outward reality, crystallized in the immobility of the moment, underlines and parallels the intense but restrained, almost hidden life. In this self-contained expression of a complete organic unity, the artist, certain of the reality he has reconstructed, asks for neither understanding nor participation on the part of the viewer.

PETER PAUL RUBENS
Siegen 1577—Antwerp 1640
*The Arrival of Marie de' Medici at Marseilles* (1622–25) Panel; 155 1/2″ × 116 1/4″. It is one of the twenty-one historical-mythological scenes on the *Life of Marie de' Medici* commissioned from the artist by the Queen of France for the Luxembourg Palace in 1622, all of them completed within four years, in an almost miraculous burst of activity.

*Above:*

FRANS HALS
Antwerp circa 1581–85—Haarlem 1666
*The Gypsy* (circa 1630)
Panel: 22 3/4″ × 20 1/2″.

*Right:*

JOHANNES VERMEER
Delft 1632–1675
*The Lace Maker* (circa 1665)
Panel; 9 1/2″ × 8 1/4″.
Signed at the upper right on the very light background with a slightly darker color.

*Left:*

REMBRANDT VAN RIJN
Leyden 1606—Rozengracht 1669
*The Supper at Emmaus* (1648)
Panel; 26 3/4″ × 25 1/2″.

FRANS HALS. *The Gypsy.*
This is one of the gayest and most lively characters of that every-day world of the people and of the middle classes which Hals has set down for us: a variety of commonplace scenes expressed with the precipitous force of his imagination, with a boldness of form which seems almost fantastically modern. The brushstroke, itself modeled with skillful variations of thickness and width, impetuous yet fluid, forms the charming figure with only a few simple touches. This portrait is one of the best and most successful examples of the real character of Hals' painting. A clear, sharp light illuminates the figure from the front. The shape is formed by color relationships rather than by light and shade; each stroke expresses at the same time depth, luminosity, movement and material (this is the way Manet understood the use of the brushstroke). The laughing girl, clear and sharp as the light, seems to turn to the viewer with a spontaneity which parallels the artist's own; a spontaneity which is, however, firmly controlled by the artist's sure hand.

JOHANNES VERMEER. *The Lace Maker.*
The figure is placed in the foreground, together with all the secondary elements; it is so close to the viewer that it is difficult to pick out the forms. This is a rare type of composition for the artist, who liked to put large, empty, airy spaces between the viewer and his subject. The

ALBRECHT DÜRER
Nuremberg 1471–1528
*Self-Portrait*
Transferred from parchment to canvas, 22 1/4″ × 17 1/2″. Dated at top, 1493, and inscribed "Myn sach dy gat als es oben schtat," words perhaps in the dialect of Strasburg, meaning, "My life will go as ordered above." The flower —the "Eryngium amethystinum" —signifies loyalty and success in love. The unusual shape of the hat can be recognized in a print of the House-Book Master. Quite probably this splendid youthful self-portrait was painted during a stay in Strasburg (the artist arrived there in November, 1493) and sent to Nuremberg, where Dürer married Agnes Fry the following year, on July 7. There are two drawings which seem to be vaguely related, in Lemberg and Erlangen.

LUCAS CRANACH,
THE ELDER
Kronach 1472—Weimar 1553
*Venus in a Landscape* (1529)
Detail
Panel; 15″ × 10 1/4″.
Signed and dated in the lower right hand corner.

placement of the light source to the right is also rare. On the other hand, the low angle of vision, here emphasized by the way the figure is cut off and fitted into the frame, was frequently used by the artist. Both theme and subject are from contemporaneous or earlier genre painters. The extraordinarily "impressionistic" technique and the formal technique in general point to a familiarity with earlier and contemporaneous figurative traditions (for example, Velazquez). But every historical reference, every traditional element, immediately loses its identity in Vermeer's personality. He is always able to see and to record the unchangeable and inexpressible beauty in everything, the eternal delight of those moments of absolute reality which men are able to feel only rarely, and then never so clearly, strongly and permanently as in his work. In few other works are his exceptional sensibility so realized.

ALBRECHT DÜRER. *Self-Portrait.*
Students of iconology have long been interested in this painting because of the hat, the inscription and especially the jewel-like flower which the twenty-two year-old Dürer holds in his right hand. According to scholars, the fact that the picture was painted specifically as love-token explains its sensuous refinement and the absence of dramatics.

A certain softness still models the bony face and strong features. The hair falls in disordered locks; the beard is only a hint of thin, blond fuzz; the magnificent dress shows a desire to adopt exotic costumes. Yet in this youthful image there is already a remarkable impressiveness. The artist's self-assurance is underlined by his self-possessed posture, turned diagonally towards the dark background, as well as by the strength of a basic composition only superficially graceful and naturalistic, and by the force of a style which has already developed beyond the Italian and German tradition which first inspired it. The most interesting detail is that of the hands, which seem about to open, especially the right one, with a slow, unfolding movement like the opening of a flower. These are the powerful instruments of the artist.

LUCAS CRANACH, the Elder. *Venus in a Landscape.*
This is one of a number of paintings of a similar subject, varying only slightly the linear rhythm of the graceful body, twisting in a slow, spiral movement about its own axis, and the few, bright details, such as the border of the invisible veil, the hair and the necklace. Differences of background and of allegorical elements are more important. This Venus is not one of the most famous, but is certainly one of the most interesting, and one of the best examples of Flemish influence on the artist's style, an influence which is still evident after 20 year's absence. It can be seen not only in the weightlessness and lack of real movement of the body, in contrast to the classic or Italian volumetric style, and in the landscape to the right which looks logical and "real," but also in the minute, detailed rendering of the abstract arabesque of the pebbles, the metallic curls of her locks, the bright, sudden glints from the dark trees; and in the colors, too, even though they have been consciously kept down to a few basic tones. The influence of Italian art, perhaps Botticelli, though remote, is reflected in the rhythm of the silhouette. Here a feeling for nature and atmosphere, which caused Cranach to be

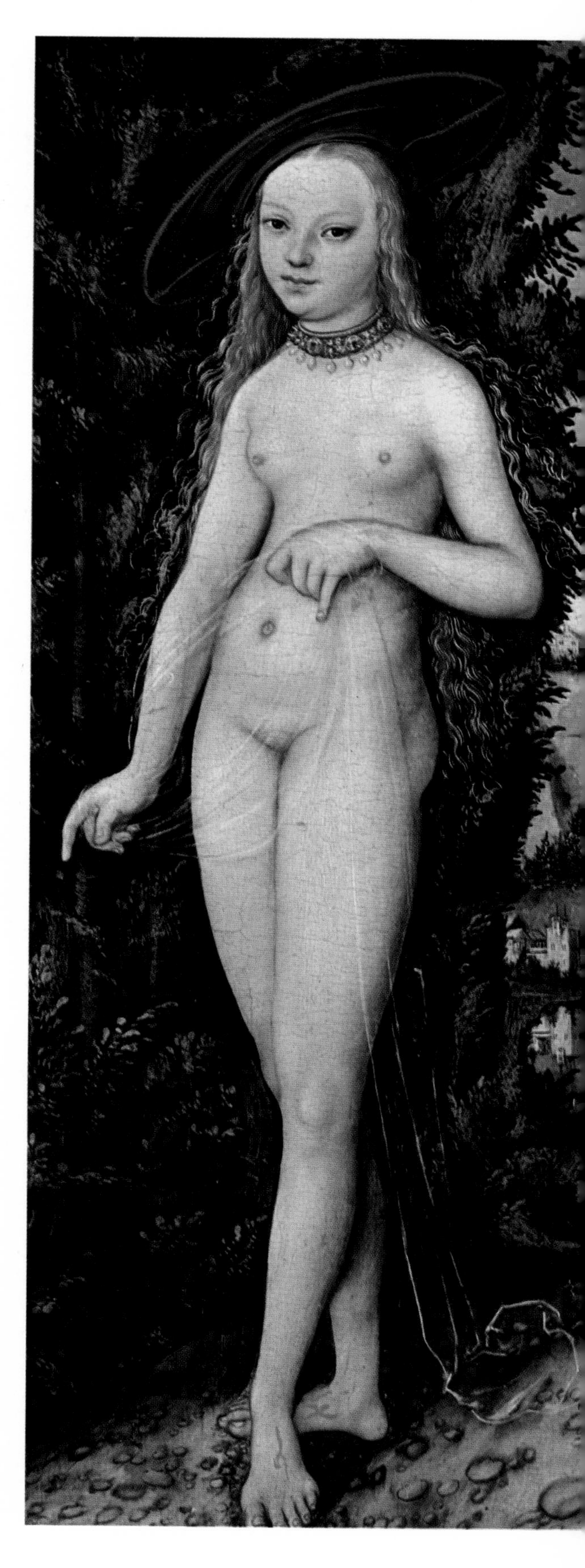

called a precursor of Brueghel, is emphasized. There is more life in this brief expanse of mournful forest, and in the representation of the background landscape than in the sinuous form of the central figure.

EL GRECO. *St. Louis, King of France, with a Page.*
There are mysterious elements in the figure of this ascetic monarch, identified by some scholars as the saintly King Ferdinand of Spain. The painting belongs to the most mature phase of the artist's activity in Spain. At this time the experience of his study in Italy, and especially his study of Titian and Tintoretto, had already long been incorporated in his painting after his arrival in Spain in 1577.

He has gone beyond all these influences, fusing them in what has been called Greco's a-naturalist, anti-naturalist or even supernatural style. This is a manner which, even in a limited and strictly defined subject like this portrait, manages to give to the image a profound spiritual meaning, detaching it from any reference to day-to-day existence. The artist achieves this more by reversing every law of geometry, of perspective and of gravity, by ignoring every system of proportions, than by the consciously ambiguous, enigmatic significance of his subject matter. The enormous shoulder and the arm held out on the left bring forward the whole weight of the main figure, which is placed on a slant. The page is simply fitted in, without either weight or relief, in order to complete a composition which avoids symmetric and emphatic structure. The painting is devoid of any indication of real space; the column in the background, with its very high base, does not, nor is it meant to, indicate any real building. It serves only to emphasize the descending and forward movement of the figures. Within this non-existent space, in the empty silence of the dark background, Greco's miraculous colors are as much an "internal" element as the light which falls on the group from the foreground. The colors sparkle, breathe, touch every form, as they create a vision beyond and above the reality of the story.

DIEGO VELAZQUEZ DE SILVA. *The Infanta Margarita.*
The age of the Infanta provides us with a precise date for this portrait, painted during Velazquez' most brilliant period at the Court in Madrid. There he was involved in an intense activity which inevitably led him to devote himself to official commissions, and which often forced him, overburdened as he was by commissions, to use assistants instead of carrying out all the work himself.

He did not use assistants for this painting, however. It is one of his most personal works, in which his painting is at its most spontaneous and has the immediacy and honesty characteristic of all the authentic work of this master. The lofty official subject has been transformed into this little princess, whose typical Bourbon features are intentionally played down. The figure is at once moving and imposing by the boldness of the brilliant effects of color on her dress and in the background, only barely hinted at, as well as by the atmosphere of fragile, childish softness which the vibrant, almost evanescent light brings to her face and to the shining, delicately soft, blond hair.

FRANCISCO DE GOYA Y LUCIENTES
Fuentedetodos 1764—Bordeaux 1828
*Doña Rita of Barrenechea, Marquesa de la Solana and Condesa del Carpio* (circa 1794–95)
Oil on canvas: 72″ × 48 3/4″.

FRANCISCO DE GOYA Y LUCIENTES. *Doña Rita of Barranechea, Marquesa dela Solana and Condesa del Carpio.* *(See page 160)*
Painted in the artist's mature period, this figure is outstanding in its simplicity and aloofness among the large series of splendid, very "Spanish" portraits which represent the more serene aspect of Goya's style. This is not the Goya involved with anguish, cruelty, misery and the injustice of life doubtless the basic themes of his work, to be found not only in his wonderful drawings and famous prints, but also in his painting. Yet, even in this other, calm view of the world, one which delights in beauty and delicacy, elegance and wit, Goya's strength affirms itself. All attention is centered on the slender figure, dominating an empty space with scarcely any background. The artist concentrates on the splendid, fantastic color contrast of the dress, the deep, intense black, as soft as a butterfly's wing, and of the veil and luminous hair-ribbon; a contrast effectively repeated by the black mass of unruly hair framing the pale face.

EL GRECO
(DOMENICO THEOTOCOPOULOS)
Crete 1531–Toledo 1614
*St. Louis, King of France, with a Page*
(1586–96)
Panel; 46″ × 37 1/2″

DIEGO VELAZQUEZ DE SILVA
Seville 1599—Madrid 1660
*The Infanta Margarita* (circa 1653)
Oil on canvas; 50 1/2″ × 39 1/4″.

# HISTORY OF THE MUSEUM AND ITS BUILDING

# HISTORY OF THE COLLECTIONS

On July 27, 1793 the "Musée central des Arts" was established by decree of the Revolutionary Government and less than a month later it was open to the public in the Grande Galerie of the Louvre. Though it actually included only a small selection of paintings from the incredibly rich collection of the former king, it was greeted by the people with tremendous enthusiasm. It was carried out by the Convention, but plans for it had been under way long before, under the monarchy, influenced by new situations and points of view which had developed in the context of the culture of the Enlightenment. Such eighteenth-century projects are evidence of a new consciousness of the possible historical and educational importance of these collections, gathered together through hundreds of years by the kings of France, from whom they were now inherited, along with the palace that housed them. In tracing their formation, as objects were bought, received as gifts or confiscated, we trace also a pattern of the tastes which marked four hundred years of French, as well as European art.

The first nucleus of the collection can be traced back to Francis I (1515–1547), who gathered together paintings, sculptures and other objects which reflect the tone of his court, at once learned and sophisticated; almost pedantic, almost frivolous. At that time he, perhaps more than any other Northern ruler, was open to the currents of innovation coming in from the South. Upon his return from his military campaigns around Milan he chose Fontainebleau as his residence, and invited artists, such masters as Leonardo, Rosso Fiorentino and Benvenuto Cellini—the greatest of their time—to France. He added to his collection works by Titian, Fra' Bartolomeo, Raphael, Sebastiano del Piombo, and the last year of his life he had the construction of the Louvre begun on the Right Bank of the Seine on the site of a thirteenth-century fortress.

The building project was carried on during the rest of the century, but the royal collections did not grow much under the following kings. This fact reflects the grave political crisis France was undergoing in the second half of the sixteenth century. Louis XIII was not himself an enthusiastic collector, but he was fortunate in having as his minister Cardinal Richelieu, a true art lover and collector—an *amateur* in the seventeenth-century meaning of the word. Richelieu acquired for the king such works as Leonardo's *Madonna and St. Anne,* the huge *Supper at Emmaus* by Veronese and a ceiling panel by his friend Poussin representing the *Allegory of Time and Truth.* At this time the Queen Mother, Marie de' Medici, who was then involved in building her own palace in the Luxembourg Gardens, also commissioned various works, such as the well-known suite of canvases by Rubens, now on exhibit at the Louvre. In spite of this, according to Villot and Engerand, when Louis XIV came to the throne the whole collection amounted to only slightly over 200 paintings. But at the death of Louis XIV, the collection consisted of 2,000 paintings; a tremendous growth which marks the most brilliant half-century of French collecting. From the beginning of his long reign, the king and his minister, Cardinal Mazarin, planned a systematic development of the royal art treasures, and they were fortunate enough to be able to buy some very important private collections, including that of Charles I, King of England. His holdings already had been enriched by the acquisition, in 1627, of most of the paintings of the Gonzagas of Mantua, a treasury of Italian Renaissance

art. When Charles's collection was dispersed, during Cromwell's revolution of 1649–50, a major part of it came into the hands of Mazarin and of Evrard Jabach, a German banker and a director of the East India Company. At Mazarin's death in 1650, Louis bought the best pieces; so Raphael's *Portrait of Baldassare Castiglione* and Correggio's *Antiope* came to the Louvre. The king bought more than 5,000 drawings and 100 paintings from Jabach, among these Giorgione's *Concert Champètre,* Caravaggio's *Death of the Virgin* and Titian's *Man with a Glove*. In 1665, too, Mazarin's grandson sold him 13 paintings by Poussin, and the same year Don Camillo Pamphili sent to Paris paintings by Albani, Annibale Carracci's *The Hunt* and *Fishing Party* and Caravaggio's *Fortune Teller*. Other gifts enriched his personal collection. From the Republic of Venice came the *Supper in the House of Simon* by Veronese, and from the collection of the landscape architect Le Nôtre came works by Claude Lorrain, Albani and Poussin.

In this way the royal gallery was filled with priceless paintings by Italian and French artists of the sixteenth and seventeenth centuries. Around the end of the century there was a renewed interest in Northern art, reflecting a new taste for intimate scenes and for domestic genre subjects, a taste which fitted into the then-modern Rococo style. All the Holbeins in the Louvre today had already been bought as part of the Jabach collection, but now Louis XIV bought such famous works as Rubens' *Kermesse* and *Self-Portrait as an Old Man.*

In the eighteenth century, the Regent, Philippe, Duc d'Orléans, was, like Louis XIV, a patron of the arts, but the collection he set up was a private one, and it was dispersed at auction after the Revolution. During the reign of Louis XV and Louis XVI the huge paintings of the previous century were less popular, because they did not fit into the delicate, intricately designed interior decoration currently fashionable. In this period the most important acquisition, in 1742, consisted of paintings from the collection of Amedeo of Savoia; these were for the most part seventeenth-century Italian paintings.

At the same time it was felt by influential people that arrangements should be made in order to organize, house and take proper care of the now huge royal collection. In 1747 a certain Lafont de Saint-Yenne passed around a petition asking for the establishment of a special gallery where young artists could study. Following this request, 110 masterpieces from the collection were exhibited in the Luxembourg in 1749: and so the first, though only temporary, public gallery in France came into being. The importance of museum studies in this period is well illustrated by Diderot's treatment of the principles underlying the organization of the collection in the Louvre, which he published in the famous *Encyclopedia* (1765). The Count of Angivillier, who became "Directeur des Bâtiments" in 1774, was in a way the creator of the museum as we know it today. Under his guidance important progress was made in planning and building the "Grande Galerie" of the palace of the Louvre. The Count also ordered some necessary restoration work, and began a policy of systematic buying, like that of Louis XIV. In these twenty years were bought, for example, van Dyck's *Portrait of Charles I of England,* Rubens' *Portrait of Hélène Fourment and her Children,* Rembrandt's *Supper at Emmaus* and Ruisdael's *Sunset,* as well as works by the Le Nains, Philippe de Champaigne and the series on the *Life of St. Bruno* by Le Sueur.

It is clear that the Revolution of 1789, rather than destroying the projected museum, brought it into being. The creation took place at a time of con-

fiscation of church property and of the aristocrats who fled the country. From private collections came Michelangelo's *Slave* and Mantegna's *Allegories,* while van Eyck's *Madonna and Chancellor Rolin* and Fra' Bartolomeo's *Marriage of St. Catherine* were taken from the church of Notre-Dame at Autun. The policy of confiscations assumed alarming proportions under Napoleon, who re-named the museum after himself in 1803. In the twenty years between the Convention and the fall of his Empire, he despoiled all the conquered lands of their masterpieces, especially Italy. Italy then lost, for example, Raphael's *The Betrothal of the Virgin* and Giovanni Bellini's *Pietà.* These were the years when the Early Renaissance was being rediscovered and thus Denon, the museum's director, brought to the museum Giotto's *St. Francis Receiving the Stigmata* and Cimabue's *Madonna in Majesty* from the church of St. Francis in Pisa, among many others. This was a period of great traveling about of works of art, and many works from the so-called "central Museum" went to enrich or re-establish provincial collections. Napoleon's plan, however, collapsed when he was defeated, and already by November of 1815 more than 5,000 works of art had been returned to their respective countries: but a hundred or so masterpieces, some of which have already been mentioned, remained in the Louvre and were never returned.

In the nineteenth century, the Louvre rearranged its collections as well as engaged in buying other works. The new enthusiasm for archeology, which had started in the eighteenth century, within the context of the Neo-Classic taste, and had been encouraged by Napoleon's campaign in Egypt, caused this department to grow to international importance. It was subdivided into various departments, and the archeological collection was reorganized under Charles X. After the revolution of 1848, the whole painting collection was reorganized by Villot, who arranged it chronologically. The new emperor, Napoleon III, was ambitious in this direction, and added considerably to the Museum's holdings. In 1863 the whole Campana Collection was bought. It consisted of a variety of objects and of paintings by Tura, Crivelli, Signorelli *(The Annunciation)* and Paolo Uccello *(The Battle of San Romano).* Five years later La Caze left the Louvre 800 paintings, including, among others, works by Ribera, Rembrandt, Rubens, Hals and a group of French eighteenth-century canvases (Watteau, Fragonard, Chardin) which filled an important gap, since the museum had few works of this period.

In the last hundred years, the Louvre has continued to develop. Important works such as Dürer's *Self-Portrait* and the *Pietà* of Villeneuve-les-Avignon have been bought, and to these have been added in the last six years, the *Crucifixion* by the Master of San Sebastiano, a triptych by Beccafumi, the *Flagellation* by Huguet, *Still-life with Turkey* by Ruisdael, the *Assassination of the Bishop of Liège* by Delacroix, *Young Woman with Pink* by Corot and a Turner *Landscape.* In this same period the Museum has received some splendid gifts, among them *The Card Game* by Lucas van Leyden. The Lebaudy estate and the "Amis du Louvre" have given the Museum Vouet's *Allegory: Prudence Bringing Peace and Abundance,* as well as *The Blessed Rainier Freeing the Poor from Prison in Florence* and *Young Choirboy* by Claude Vignon. Baroness Gourgaud's gift includes the *Young Woman with Mandolin* by Corot, *Don Quixote* by Daumier and *Abduction of a Young Woman* by Delacroix, as well as various Impressionist and modern works. And now that certain prejudices in taste have at last disappeared, works of the French schools of the nineteenth century and by Impressionist artists have come into the Museum through the De Béstegui, Moreau-Nélaton and Caillebotte collections.

# THE COLLECTIONS

DEPARTMENT OF GREEK AND ROMAN ANTIQUITIES
DEPARTMENT OF EGYPTIAN ANTIQUITIES
DEPARTMENT OF ORIENTAL ANTIQUITIES
DEPARTMENT OF MEDIEVAL, RENAISSANCE AND MODERN SCULPTURE
DEPARTMENT OF MEDIEVAL, RENAISSANCE AND MODERN ART OBJECTS
DEPARTMENT OF PAINTINGS AND DRAWINGS
SECTION OF CHRISTIAN ANTIQUITIES

The present Museum is divided into six Departments and a Cabinet of Drawings which gradually became separated from the nucleus of the painting collection whose history has just been traced. The Department of Greek and Roman Antiquities was the first to become autonomous. It was created in 1800, and was given its present organization in 1846. It includes, among other objects, the important group of Greek vases of the Campana Collection, the so-called "Boscoreale Treasure," composed of more than 100 pieces of Roman jewelry, given to the Museum in 1895 by Baron Rothschild, and famous works of art such as the *Venus* of Milos and the *Victory of Samothrace,* both discovered in excavations in the nineteenth century. In 1954 a "Section of Christian Antiquities" was created in order to group together Early Christian, Byzantine and Coptic works which were scattered here and there in various other departments. Aside from its Early Christian sarcophagi, Byzantine ivories, ceramics, glass, gold work and important textile collections, this Section now has also benefited from recent gifts and acquisitions, among them Greek and Russian icons and Coptic textiles.

The Department of Egyptian Antiquities was established in 1826 in order to organize Napoleon's collections. Its first curator was Champollion who first deciphered the hieroglyphs, and in this context Egyptian studies flourished. That year, "Oriental Antiquities" already formed a separate section within the Museum of ancient sculpture; in 1881 this, too, became a separate department. Organized topographically, it is exceptionally rich in Mesopotamian art, which had been brought to the Museum from the excavations at Lagash and Mari.

The "Department of Medieval, Renaissance and Modern Sculpture" was organized around what remained of the Royal Academy and its collections, moved in the Louvre in the eighteenth century. It contains Michelangelo's *Slaves,* as well as works by Cellini, Goujon, Pilon and others. It is now being enlarged to include the French eighteenth and nineteenth-century sculpture until recently kept in the storerooms. In 1893 another Department, that of Medieval, Renaissance and Modern Art Objects, was separated from this one; it includes all the precious objects from the Royal wardrobe, as well as material confiscated during the Revolution (treasures of the Order of St. Esprit, of the Royal Abbey of St. Denis and of the Ste. Chapelle), as well as the National Museum of Furniture, added to the Louvre in 1901.

# ADMINISTRATION

The enormous size of the Louvre and its collections requires a special kind of organization, one that will allow the material to be exhibited to the public and also preserved for the future in the best way possible. In the nineteenth century, the Museum became the property of the state. As part of the "Réunion des Musées Nationaux" (1896), it was run by a board, which since 1941 has been divided into two sections, financial and artistic. In this way the Museum is enriched by new acquistions, some of which are paid for by the government, others privately.

Also in the Museum are a department of restoration, a library, archives and the "Ecole du Louvre," which offers courses in art history and restoration. Attached to the Director's office is a "Service for Cultural Activities," which has, among its other responsibilities, that of organizing within the National Museums lecture tours conducted by graduates of the "Ecole du Louvre," who are selected by competitive examinations. In 1966, for example, 7,856 groups of about 25 persons visited the Louvre in this way. In 1966, again, there were 1,182,878 paying visitors, as against 589,000 in 1952. It is estimated that the number would be double if one took into account nonpaying Sunday visits and student groups. Aside from the catalogues published by the curators of the various departments, the Museum also puts out two magazines, *Le Bulletin du Laboratoire du Musée du Louvre* and *La Revue du Louvre et des Musées de France*. The Louvre regularly offers exhibitions of drawings organized by the Cabinet of drawings and also special exhibitions, like that in 1960, when 800 paintings, all of which came from the Museum's storerooms, were shown. The Department of Paintings has also, in the last few years, organized several important exhibitions abroad. In 1962, in Rome, there was "French Portraits from Clouet to Degas"; in 1965 in Canada, "Eighteenth-Century French Paintings from the Louvre"; also in 1965, in Russia, "Paintings in French Museums"; in 1966, in Japan, "'The Grand Siècle' in French Public Collections."

## THE BUILDING

Since 1939 a long-term plan has been under way to get the collections ready, so that over two hundred thousand objects can be exhibited in the Louvre. The building was certainly not constructed according to modern ideas of what a perfect museum should be; in fact, the building, like the collections, shows traces of almost four centuries of French kings, all of whom, almost without exception, made some additions to the enormous palace. The nucleus of the building goes back to Francis I. This is the south-west section of the "Square Court" or "Cour Carrée" (the plan was that of the fortress of Philippe-Auguste, which had been destroyed), designed by the architect Lescot and adorned by statues by Jean Goujon. At the beginning of the seventeenth century all the South wing of palace, along the Seine, was finished; it was planned to reach the new palace of the Tuileries on the west. In 1624 Louis XIII decided to carry out the original plan for the "Cour Carrée," to enclose it on four sides, according to plans by Lemercier. This new project was carried out from 1661–63. Then Louis XIV, who had torn down what remained of the old fortress, as well as many surrounding buildings, commissioned Le Vau to complete the "quadruplement," still basically in the style of Lescot.

These sixteenth-century plans, however, could not give the monumental effect called for by the new "Porte d'Honneur" of the east side. The minister Colbert, therefore, ignoring the plans of Le Vau, Lemercier and Mansart, called in Bernini from Rome. In 1665, Bernini presented a baroque plan for the long façade. This was never carried out, since the taste of Louis XIV's court was by this time more classical: the style which was typical of all the production of this artistic center in the second half of the seventeenth century was already flowering. The suggestion put forward by a committee, Perrault, Le Vau and Le Brun, to have a long, continuous colonnade with a single row of columns, was taken up, and the façade was carried out along the south side of the palace as well. The decorations Le Brun executed for the "Petite Galerie" and in the rooms of the "Colonnade" also belong to this period.

When Louis XIV settled permanently in Versailles in 1678 the work had not yet been finished, and the palace was nearly abandoned. It was used only for meetings of the Academy, as a residence for members of the court, for offices and storerooms. Only at the end of the century, with the future Museum in mind, work started again under the supervision of the architects Gabriel and Soufflot. It was left to Napoleon to complete Perrault's "Cour Carrée" and "Colonnade" in the early years of the nineteenth century, as well as a wing on the north, along the Rue de Rivoli. The latter was continued by Napoleon III, fifty years later. He hired the architects Le Fuel and Visconti in an effort to make the west side, at last, harmonize with the whole. But when the work of so many centuries was finished at last, the palace of the Tuileries, ironically enough, burned down in 1871; and the original plan, to have a single complex, tied to the façade of the palace in a unified perspective, was never realized.

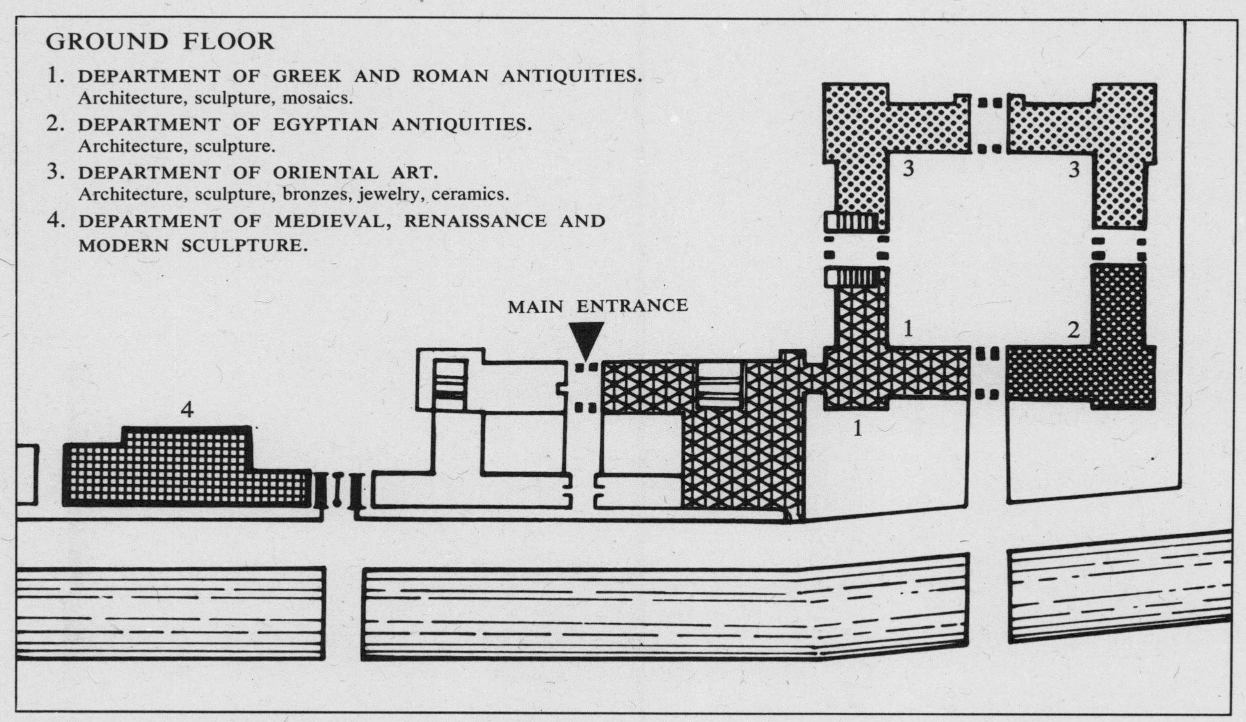




Plans of the Museum: Editions Musées Nationaux, Service des Activités Culturelles, Paris.

## SECOND FLOOR

1. DEPARTMENT OF GREEK AND ROMAN ANTIQUITIES.
   Bronzes, jewelry, ceramics, Etruscan art.
2. DEPARTMENT OF EGYPTIAN ANTIQUITIES.
   Art objects.
3. DEPARTMENT OF ORIENTAL ART.
   Islamic Room.
4. DEPARTMENT OF MEDIEVAL, RENAISSANCE AND MODERN ART OBJECTS.
   Treasures of the French kings, furniture, bronzes, tapestries, porcelains, jewelry.
5. THE "GRANDE GALERIE."

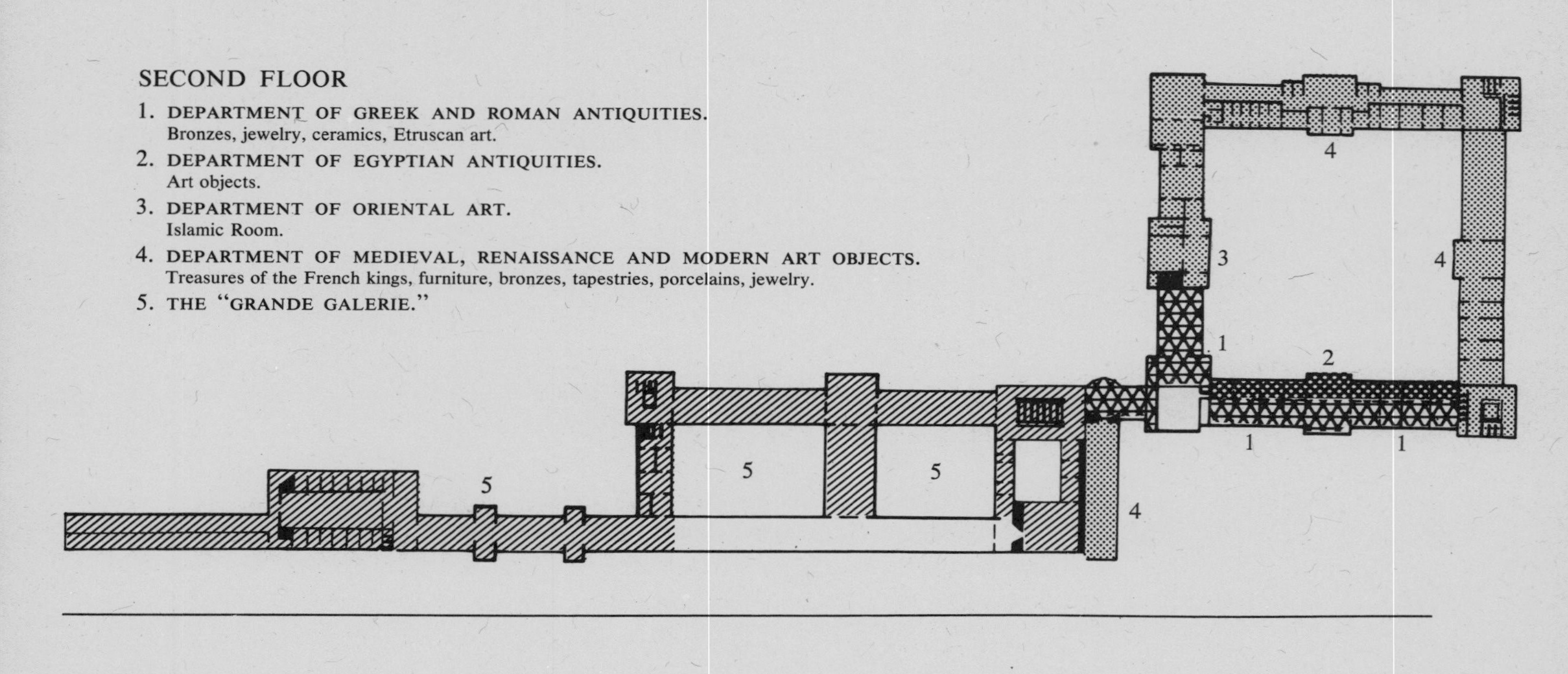

## "GRANDE GALERIE"—FIRST FLOOR

DEPARTMENT OF PAINTING

1. Italy
2. France and Spain, 17th century
3. Flanders
4. Rubens (Life of Marie de' Medici)
5. France and Netherlands, from 14th to 16th centuries
6. Holland, 17th century
7. France, 19th century

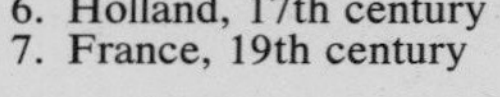

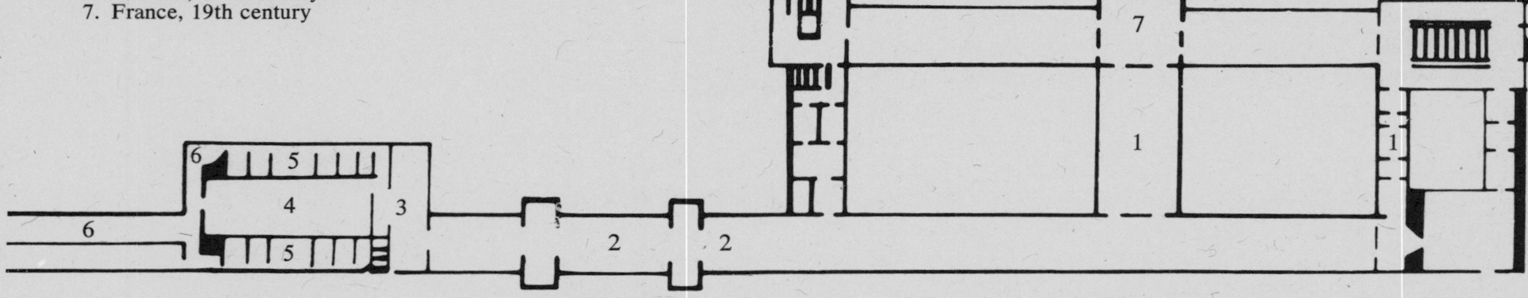

## LEGEND

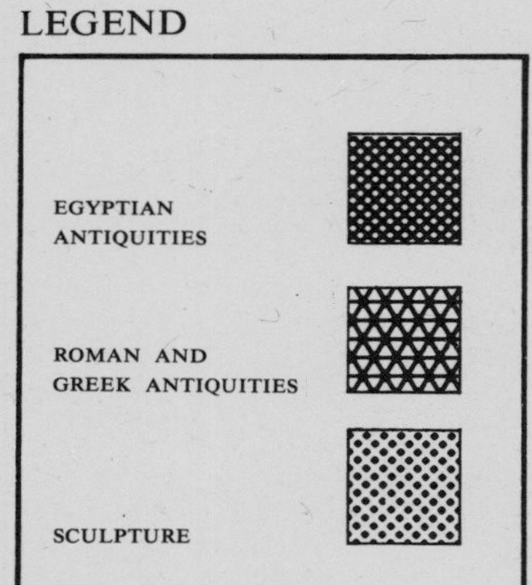


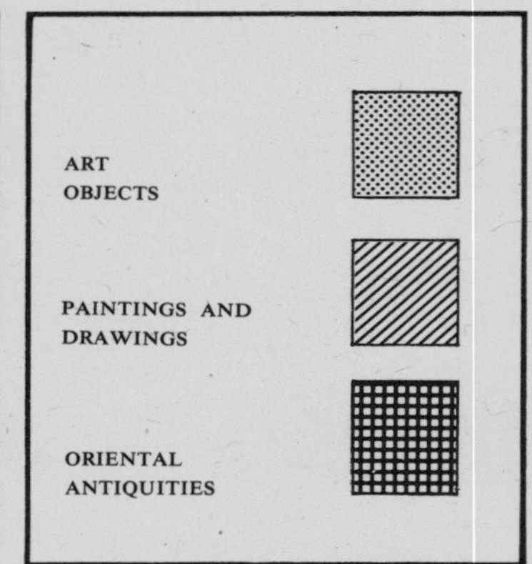


## "GRANDE GALERIE"—SECOND FLOOR

1. 18th-century Painting
2. 19th-century Painting

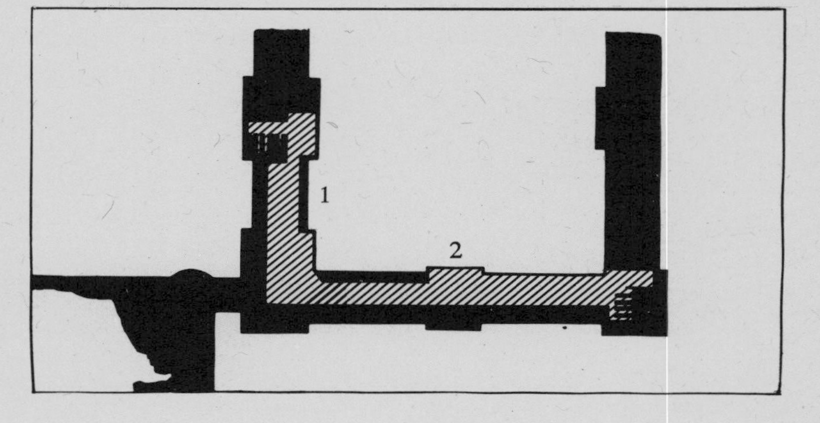

# SELECTED BIBLIOGRAPHY


SMITH, WILLIAM STEVENSON: *The Art & Architecture of Ancient Egypt.* (Pelican History of Art, Penguin Books, Baltimore, 1958).

ALDRED, CYRIL: *Development of Ancient Egyptian Art, 3200–1315 B.C.* (Tiranti, London, 1952).

FRANKFORT, HENRI: *The Art and Architecture of the Ancient Orient.* (Pelican History of Art, Penguin Books, Baltimore, 1955).

CHAMOUX, FRANÇOIS: *Greek Art.* (In the Pallas Library of Art, New York Graphic Society, Greenwich, Connecticut).

BIEBER, MARGARETE: *The Sculpture of the Hellenistic Age.* (Columbia University Press New York).

VOLBACH, W. F.: *Early Christian Art, the Late Renaissance & Byzantine Empires from the 3rd to the 7th Centuries.* (Abrams, New York).

BURCKHARDT, JAKOB, C.: *The Civilization of the Renaissance.* (3rd rev. ed., Phaidon, London, 1950).

CHASTEL, ANDRÉ: *The Flowering of the Renaissance.* (Odyssey Press, New York).

DEWALD, ERNEST T.: *Italian Painting, 1200–1600.* (Holt, Rinehart & Winston, New York, 1961).

WATERHOUSE, ELIS: *Italian Baroque Painting.* (Phaidon, London & New York, 1961).

PANOFSKY, E.: *Early Netherlandish Painting.* (Harvard University Press, 1954).

FRIEDLÄNDER, MAX: *From Van Eyck to Brueghel.* (Phaidon, 1956).

BENESCH, OTTO: *The Art of the Renaissance in Northern Europe.* (Harvard University Press, 1945).

FROMENTIN, EUGÈNE: *The Masters of Past Times, Dutch and Flemish Painting.* (Phaidon, London, 1948).

BURCKHARDT, JAKOB C.: *Recollections of Rubens,* tr. By Mary Hottinger (Oxford University Press, New York, 1950).

WILENSKI, R. H.; *Dutch Painting.* (The Beechhurst Press, New York, 1955).

ROSENBERG, JAKOB: *Rembrandt.* (Harvard University Press, 1948).

JEDLICKA, GOTTHARD: *Spanish Painting.* (Viking Press, New York, 1963).

CHÂTELET, ALBERT AND THUILLIER, JACQUES: *French Painting, from Fouquet to Poussin.*

CHÂTELET, ALBERT AND THUILLIER, JACQUES: *French Painting from LeNain to Fragonard.*

JEAN LEYMARIE: *French Painting, the 19th Century.* (Skira, Geneva and New York).

FRIEDLAENDER, WALTER F.: *From David to Delacroix.* (Harvard University Press, 1952).

REWALD, JOHN: *History of Impressionism.* (Museum of Modern Art, New York 1946).

REWALD, JOHN: *Post-Impressionism from Van Gogh to Gauguin.* (Museum of Modern Art, New York, 1956).


---


*For their courtesy in furnishing information relating to their departments we wish to thank Michel Lacotte, Head Curator of the Department of Paintings; Jean David Weill of the Moslem Art Section of the Department of Oriental Antiquities; Etienne Coche de la Ferté of the Section of Christian Antiquities; Pierre Amiet of the Department of Oriental Antiquities; R. Antelme of the Department of Egyptian Antiquities.*

# INDEX OF ILLUSTRATIONS

# INDEX OF NAMES

*Note: Italic numbers refer to names mentioned in captions.*

# GENERAL INDEX